Live Below Your Means:The Art of Living With Very Little Money

(Occasionally illustrated of course.)

By Micah Coulter

Disclaimer

What you do with this information is your legal responsibility.

The author or publisher **is NOT** responsible in any way for any loss of life, any crime committed, any injury, loss of wealth, damage to property, or anything else that may occur when using the information in this book. Don't buy something or do something because this guide suggests it and then blame the book.

If you don't like an idea, don't follow it!

Use your own common sense and personal tastes as this guide is only for informational purposes.

Contents

Everyday Cheap Living — 9

Save Money on Low Income — 12

Save Money on Food — 15

Cheap Recipes — 35

Save Money on Hygiene — 43

Save Money on Cleaning Supplies — 49

Save Money on Clothing — 55

Save Money on Utilities/Doing without — 61

Save Money on Shelter — 67

Save money on Furniture — 71

Save money on Home Security — 73

Save Money on Transportation — 90

Save Money on Entertainment — 93

Save Money on Healthcare — 96

Income without a Job — 98

Save money on Losing Weight — 101

Passive Income — 107

The Art of Free and Recycling — 126

Homesteading On Breadcrumbs 137

The Slingshot for Survival and Sport 145

Frugal Troubleshooting 148

The Frugal Shopping List 154

Conclusion 157

"Poverty is more a state of mind than an economic condition. If you have the will to survive you will live quite well, no matter what the economic conditions."
- Edward H. Romney

Introduction

If you've lost your job, you're struggling to pay bills, been laid off, live on a fixed income, or are living on a single income: you've now found the book to help you make changes in your life. In this book, we'll discuss all the little details from homemade cleaning supplies and hygiene products to learning how to improvise items and save money on groceries.

From a former homeless man's perspective:
You don't have to have a ton of money to be happy. Some of the richest people in the world are depressed and miserable.
Why? You thought with all that cash and the ability to do whatever they wanted would always make them happy? Why are they not? Don't look at money as the answer for your happiness. A lot of people have too much of it, and they are never happy.

Remember:
The best things in life aren't what money can buy,
but the simplest of things which cannot be bought,
like health and well being.
Learning to enjoy the small things in life is where
the true wealth lies. The morning rain, a warm cup
of tea in the winter, playing with a warm little puppy;
that makes life good.
Don't let money get you down, as it was always
meant to be spent. Money comes and goes, but
your time cannot. You have this one single life on
earth that you'll never have again, why spend it
chasing a piece of paper?

Life will throw curveballs and will knock you down.
Get back up with a smile and remember that the
key to happiness is being present in the moment.
Yes, you're in debt but so is everybody; that's how
this system works. You're in debt from your
eighteenth birthday until the very day you die. You'll
never pay it all off no matter what you do, so don't
stress too much about it.

You might be thinking, "Sure, I can pay all my
debts." Even if you own your own home, vehicle,
yacht, or whatever- you're still in debt to the
government by taxation on those items. Debt is
unavoidable, so don't prioritize it above your family
and your well being.
There are people the world over who have gotten
by with less, and so can we. We don't have to live

lavish lifestyles. You can have your cake and eat it too.

Starting out, take a look at all the items you have around you. If you're like anybody else in these modern times, you likely have a large HD television, nice clothes that you bought brand new, and maybe a few subscriptions to video apps that you rarely use except on the weekends when you're not slaved to death at your job. Then just like myself and everyone else, you have the audacity to complain as to why you can't make ends meet. People are on antidepressant medications and stressed out of their minds despite having all this luxury. Do you know why? Money. Bills. Debt.

They try to go out and numb the pain with alcohol. Some turn to drugs, others turn to eating. Most sit and stare at screens to distract themselves from the absurdity of it all.

Everyone is looking to feel something again, and no matter who you are; you escape one way or another. Either by hobby or drugs, food or pills; caught in the cycle of working just enough to feel free, but feeling too tired to be anything but complacent at the end of the work day. Where is the logic in this lifestyle?

Here's the solution to those problems in one simple statement: live below your means.

My grandfather Joe sat me down one day as a young man and gave me some advice.

"If you want to save money, you've got to live below your means." I didn't grasp what he meant by that then, but I've come along way since that time. Ask yourself this: did you really need that overly expensive HD television with 1080p resolution, that wall mount kit, and those surround sound speakers? Of course not. Sure, you worked for it. Sure, you can do as you please.
But as you sit there staring at all that, be honest with yourself. What would you rather be doing?

In a quote from Charles Long, "Who said ambition has to come from your job?"

Everyday Cheap Living

Get up with a game plan

Wake up in the morning with gratitude and intention. Most successful people start the day with intention. Either you'll accomplish something today, or you'll achieve something. It doesn't have to be elaborate, it could be as simple as going grocery shopping.

Unplug unnecessary appliances

One of the first things my wife and I do is unplug our phone chargers after getting out of bed. Those things basically sit around drawing unused power. This can be applied to nearly everything in your house. Hair dryers, fans, televisions, stoves, coffee pots, air conditioners, game systems, washers and dryers, etc.

I practiced this routine daily for an entire month. I unplugged everything that wasn't in use, minus the refrigerator.

I saw a decrease in my monthly electricity bill by $4.00!

Eat lightly

Unless medical conditions prevent you from skipping meals or otherwise, consider eating something very light for breakfast. It could be a banana and a cup of coffee. It could be a bowl of oatmeal and a cup of tea: anything that you can eat.

For lunch and dinner, make only what you will eat. Usually in portioned amounts. Keep any leftovers for a meal the next day. Don't throw away your leftovers or keep them with only the intention of eating them. The only thing that results from that is rotten food and wasted money.

On coffee or tea

Limit yourself to one cup a day. It'll save you a lot of money in the long run as opposed to heavy coffee drinkers. Both of these beverages are luxuries and expensive ones at that. Just one cup. If the stuff in the pot is a few hours old, drink it anyway. Your fellow man worked hard to produce that coffee for you.

You and cheap living

It's up to you to pinch every penny and learn to be resourceful. This guide is expansive, but none of this information is going to do you any good if you don't have a little self control. It's hard when you go out to the store to buy something, and then you end up coming home with five things you didn't need and a new shirt they had on clearance.
You have to have control of yourself if you're ever to succeed in saving.
Cheap living is a way of life, and it can be tiresome trying to pinch every little penny you can get.
Still, that's a penny you can put back and save.
One-hundred pennies is a whole dollar.
Think about it.

Your Dignity
Just because you're poor doesn't mean you have to show it. You could bathe regularly, You could wear secondhand clothes, work a minimum wage job, eat healthy, and look middle class: all on less than $1,400 a month.
You don't eat from trash cans just because you're poor. You can get comfortably by on barely anything if you do the math and play your cards right. Even if you did dig something out of a dumpster, it doesn't make you any less of a human being. We all have to survive regardless, and we're all worthy of love.
The best part about having barely anything is that it makes you rich both mentally and spiritually. You wake up with less bills to worry about. You spend less time at the office; you just work eight hours and done.
Sure, the work is hard; yet you're thankful to the powers that may be for your opportunity to provide for yourself.
Being poor does not take away your dignity. If anything, having very little in wealth means you have much more wealth in another greater sense. That's the beauty of cheap living.

Save Money on Low Income

Save a little money each paycheck
Besides not spending any money other than what is utmost necessary (Ex. Utilities, Rent, Insurance,

Groceries) and saving what you can, you can amass a large sum of money over time. In order to save money, you must first sit down and distinguish the money from which you can spend and from which you cannot. You must find your monthly wage. In order to do that use the math formulas provided below. *Gross* means a sum without taxes factored.

Ex:
1. *Hourly income x hours worked in a week = 1 weeks wages (gross)*
2. *Weekly wages x 4 (four weeks in a month)= monthly wage (gross)*
3. *Monthly wage x 12 = annual wage (gross)*

Determine the sum of all your bills for each month. Subtract the amount from your monthly wage.

Ex:
1. *Monthly wage - bills = potential savings*
2. *Potential savings - grocery budget = savings*

Whatever money you have leftover after deducting the sum of your bills from your monthly wage, can be further deducted from by your grocery budget (I'll help you determine your budget in the next chapters) to produce what I like to call "savings". Basically it's money that you could do absolutely anything with, but should save.

Place the money "savings" into a savings account at your preferred bank.

You'll continue to do these math calculations every single month to determine what you can potentially save so that you can actually do it.

As you know, your pay could fluctuate depending on whether or not you get sick, skip work, call off or just work less hours.

Do you have any bad habits?

I'd advise if you are trying to save money and have any unnecessary bad habits, to do away with them. After all, they are the reason you're struggling to get ahead, whether realized or not. They are taking a chunk of your money. Calculate using the formula below if you don't believe me.

Ex:
1. *Bad habit price x amount consumed per week = weekly expense*
2. *Weekly expense x 4 (four weeks in a month) = monthly expense*
3. *Monthly expense x 12 (twelve months in a year) = annual expense*

Unfortunately, you'll have to further deduct the monthly expense of your bad habit from the potential savings.

Ex:
1. *Potential savings - monthly expense = savings*

Whatever is the difference between the expense and potential savings is what you'll be able to save each month.

Save Money on Food

Make a household item list

Every item you use in the house including food should be written on a piece of paper. Go over the checklist weekly with each individual item, and decide what you do and don't need for the rest of this week.

Are you out of something or not?

If you are almost out of something or already out, write it down on your grocery list for that week. If you have enough of something and you don't see running out of it within the next week, don't write it down.

Don't shop hungry

Going in to the grocery store hungry is asking to overspend. You're likely to be more impulsive and not think things through when you're hungry. Grab a quick bite at home before heading out.

Don't "dine out"

Even if it's only a dollar spent. The food you have at home is more than enough, plus your already spent money on it.

Make a list and stick to it
Develop an affordable and rational grocery list
suited to your diet, and stick to it. Try to keep it as
healthy as possible. Avoid pre-made food and
heavily processed foods. Stick to whole foods.

Buy only generic
Name brand foods are more expensive, and it's the
same thing you get if you buy generic. I have found
that generic items seem to sometimes have more
chemicals, but this is only an assumption I've
developed from comparing food labels.

Make a grocery budget
Name a price, and find a way to fit what you need
around it. Avoid buying anything that's not on the
list and shop with a calculator if you have to.

Shop at $1 stores for household needs
$1 stores are great for finding household dishes
and some cooking utensils all for just 1.00. You can
even decorate an entire house with some of the
items you can find in a $1 store.

Affordable supermarkets and salvage
Find the store in your area with the best food deals
related to your grocery list and then buy them.
Salvage stores are also best if you find any in your
area.

Use a calculator when shopping
My clever wife taught me this. How in the hell I
didn't think of it before is beyond me.
Simply take a calculator in the store with you with
your budget entered.
As you add each item to the cart, deduct its store
price from your budget until you are left with no
more money.
At that point, decide what is necessary and what
you can do without that week.
This keeps everything down to basics and allows
you to stick to your budget.

Pay with cash
Similar to the calculator idea. Go into the store with
a set amount of money in cash and make your
groceries fit to that amount.
Can be slightly embarrassing if you miscalculate
and have to put something back at the register.

No junk food or sodas
Sodas and sports drinks are nothing but sugar and
unneeded calories and basically the same thing.
Even the diet kind are often full of chemicals.
I personally haven't drank a soda in over 7 years,
as they are terrible for the kidneys. Drink water
instead. You'll save money and actually be putting
something in your body that it was meant to filter.
Your kidneys will thank you later in life too.

As for the junk food, you can treat yourself
occasionally, but don't live off of the stuff. It's often

full of sugar, salt, and unnatural oils. Yes, it's usually cheap.
The real cost is your health from years of eating it and you end up with a big medical bill.
Everything in moderation.

Weekly checklist

Go over your grocery list and determine what you do have and don't have. If almost out or out of, add to shopping list. If you still have half or more, wait until next week.

Buy clearance

Check the clearance section every time you go to the store and try to make a habit of it.
Often you may find good deals on stuff you normally buy if you are diligent. If you find something that you use a lot of, be sure and buy extra so that you'll pay less for it in the long run.

Can your own food

If you have the know how and some mason jars, you can can your own food that you grow in the garden and preserve it for later.
You can make homemade jellies, jams, soups and whatever else and simply can them and save them for later. A great way to save money, especially when cooking large pots of beans and then canning them for later. Be sure and mark the date you canned them on a label and place it on the jar somewhere. Don't eat very old cans of food, and if you do, be sure it's sealed properly.

Live off the land

Something my grandmother did all her life and taught me how to do as a young boy was gardening. Through it, you feel closer to the earth. It teaches you many life lessons, like patience and responsibility: especially during the summer droughts. We typically had to water all the plants by hand because we had no rain. It taught me to respect and care for other living beings, and in return they fed me with their fruits and vegetables.

Not only can you grow a garden, but you can also learn to eat wild edibles and how to identify them. This is risky because if you misidentify a plant that has a poisonous look alike, you could get gravely sick or worse.
Luckily Dandelions are easy to remember and are good for you. There are several plants out there that have no known look alikes and are incredibly healthy to eat.

And while we're on the subject, yes you can also can wild edibles.

Hunting/Fishing

You can take up hunting and fishing both as a peaceful past time and a way to put meat on the table.

Learning to process your own meat and preserving it can be a rewarding experience and make you feel as though you're in touch with the earth.

Personally, I don't believe in hunting for sport; and no, I do NOT enjoy it. Taking the life of another living being for food is nothing enjoyable.

Personally, I believe if you're going to hunt it, then you should eat it. If you're not going to eat something, don't deny it of it's right to live.

I rarely hunt anymore as I do not see the need for it. These days my diet is mostly vegetarian. Mainly because meat is too expensive; the other reason being I don't like meat.

Dumpster dive

I used to hitchhike from town to town and I did so living entirely by what I found in the dumpsters of local stores.

Weekly, stores throw out all kinds of food, clothing, electronics and all sorts of other goodies that are ripe for the picking. Sometimes you get lucky and sometimes you don't.

Dumpster diving is dangerous and you could easily get injured so only do it if your life depends on it. Also, don't mess with enclosed dumpsters or any dumpster that has locks. You could be charged with breaking and entering or trespassing and end up doing jail time.

You also don't know why the food was thrown away. Often it's just because it's close to the expiration date.

There is sometimes a chance that it was thrown out because there is a safety recall, and eating it could make you deathly sick.

Try to keep up to date on safety recalls if you can.

If it's not locked and not on private property, then have at it.

You know the risks, don't be careless!

Wild edibles

Nature provides natural foods for us as well. These are the most common wild edibles in Eastern North America and are quite easy to identify.

NEVER EAT ANY PLANT WITHOUT KNOWING ALL OF THE POSSIBLE RISKS.
DO NOT EAT A PLANT WITHOUT POSITIVELY IDENTIFYING IT.
PLANTS ON THIS LIST MAY REQUIRE EXTRA PREPARATION TO BECOME EDIBLE.
SOME PLANTS MAY BE TOXIC UNLESS COOKED.
IT IS YOUR RESPONSIBILITY TO DETERMINE WHAT IS SAFE TO EAT.
IF YOU ARE UNSURE, DON'T EAT IT.

Dandelion (Taraxacum Officinale)

source:
https://commons.wikimedia.org/wiki/Category:Taraxacum_officinale#/media/File:Dandelion_(3483575184).jpg

Edible: Leaves, roots and flower. Roasted root acts as coffee substitute. <u>Too much consumption acts as a laxative</u>. Roots and leaves can be dried and stored and used as tea.
Locations: Waste Areas, lawns, roadsides, fields, wood margins, virtually everywhere.

source:https://commons.wikimedia.org/wiki/Category:Taraxacum_officin
ale#/media/File:Taraxacum_officinale_plant1_(16376722765).jpg

source:https://commons.wikimedia.org/wiki/Category:Taraxacum_offici
nale#/media/File:Taraxacum_officinale_plant6_(16375803122).jpg

Wood Sorrel (*Oxalis stricta*)

source:https://commons.wikimedia.org/wiki/Oxalis_stricta#/media/File:
Oxalis_stricta_flowers_and_foliage_002.JPG

Edible: Entire plant can be eaten raw or cooked.
Delicious flavor. Mildly sour. Can be used to make
tea which helps relieve indigestion in moderate
doses. Great source of vitamin C.
Astringent.

Locations: Shaded, moist soils. Often found near
wild onions, common on forest floors near the
bases of trees.

source:
https://commons.wikimedia.org/wiki/Oxalis_stricta#/media/File:Stijve_kl averzuring_Oxalis_fontana_(1).jpg

source:https://commons.wikimedia.org/wiki/Oxalis_stricta#/media/File:
Oxalis_stricta0.jpg

Broadleaf plantain (Plantago Major)

source:https://www.remedes-de-grand-mere.com/les-fondamentaux/les-plantes-medicinales/plantain/

Edible: Entire plant. Young leaves, raw or cooked.
Old leaves better cooked. Seed can be ground into meal and mixed with flour. Dried leaves make healthy tea.

Location: Grows low to the ground, common in yards, lawns, gardens, fields, meadows, pastures.

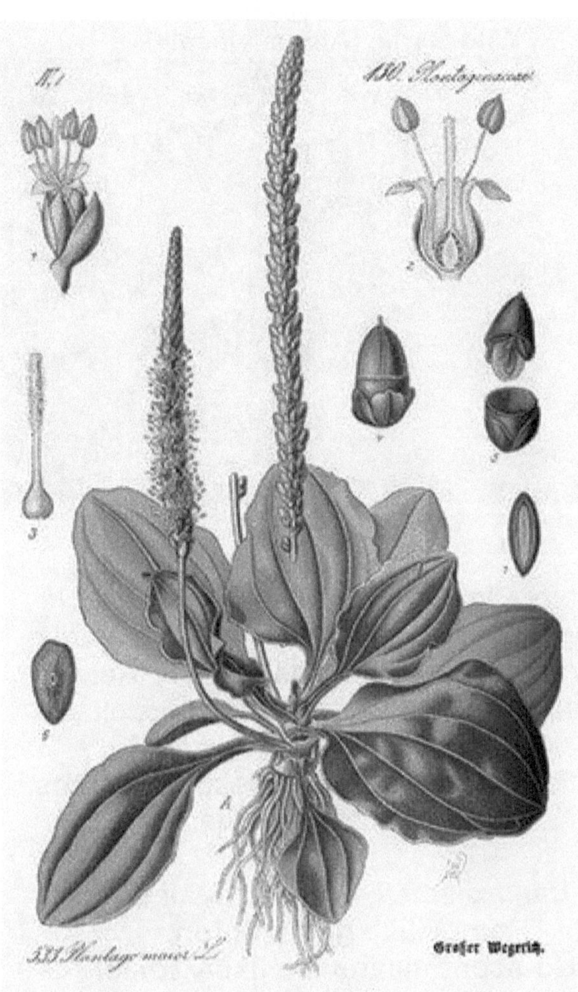

Source:
https://www.remedes-de-grand-mere.com/les-fondamentaux/les-plantes-medicinales/plantain/

Wild Garlic (Allium vineale)

source:https://commons.wikimedia.org/wiki/Allium_vineale#/media/File:
Allium_vineale_early_spring_001.JPG

Edible: Dig the tuber out of the ground. It should either have a strong onion or garlic smell. No smell means that it is likely poisonous. Can be eaten raw or cooked.

Location: Waste Ground, forest, woodlands, pretty much everywhere.

**If it has no smell, don't eat it. It should smell like garlic/onion.
No scent means it's likely toxic.**

source:https://commons.wikimedia.org/wiki/Allium_vineale#/media/File:
Allium_vineale_Pillnitz.jpg

s

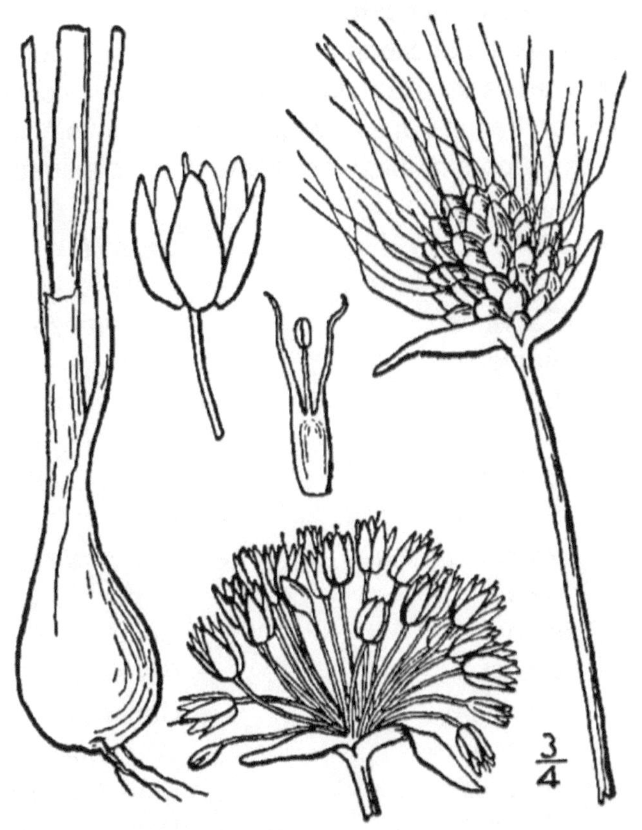

ource:https://commons.wikimedia.org/wiki/Allium_vineale#/media/File:
Allium_vineale_drawing.png

Cheap foods/Necessities

There are a lot of cheap and nutritional foods out there. Here is an example of my grocery list. Yours could be changed due to your own personal diet or allergies. Some of these are some of the cheapest foods in my opinion.

- *Russet potatoes*
- *Bananas*
- *Apples*
- *Carrots*
- *Celery*
- *Bagged Spinach*
- *Yellow Onions*
- *Sweet potatoes*
- *Green Cabbage*
- *Frozen Broccoli*
- *Old fashioned oats*
- *White rice*
- *Canned beans*
- *Eggs*
- *Peanut Butter*
- *Bakery Bread*
- *Crackers (unsalted)*
- Cucumbers
- *1% Milk*
- *Butter*
- *All purpose flour*
- *Olive oil*
- *Salt & Pepper*
- *Lemon juice*
- *Canned fruit*
- *Chocolate chips*
- *Coffee and filters/Tea*
- *Canned Vegetables*
- *Brick Cheese*
- *Whole wheat noodles*
- *Generic pasta sauce*
- *Peanuts*
- *Raisins*
- *Ramen*

Cheap Recipes

Frugal Chicken Soup
Really stretches your ingredients far and tastes amazing. Great for when you don't know what to make for supper or only have base ingredients.
Ingredients:
- *1 piece of chicken breast*
- *1 potato*
- *1 whole carrot*
- *1 onion*
- *1 celery stalk*
- *2 tablespoons of chicken bouillon*

Boil the chicken in a medium sized pot with desired amount of water. De-skin your potato and dice up your vegetables and then rinse them in a strainer with cold water. When the chicken has been boiling about 20 minutes, remove it from the pot and chop it into chunks. Careful as it will be hot. After dicing, return the chicken to the pot and add in the veggies. Now add the bouillon and let the soup boil for another 15-30 minutes, stirring occasionally. Reduce heat to low and let it cook slowly.
Soup is done when veggies are tender.
Great with bread and butter or grilled cheese!

Italian Cuisine

It'll satisfy your spaghetti craving at least.

Ingredients:

- *Whole wheat pasta*
- *Pasta sauce (of your choice)*

Boil the noodles in water with a pinch of salt and dash of olive oil. When noodles are done, strain them. Add sauce of your choice. Serve with salad and homemade garlic bread (optional).

Frugal Pizza

A really delicious and cheap way to make pizza. Dough sometimes takes longer to cook due to being raw, so cooking times vary.

Ingredients:

- *1 can biscuits*
- *1 jar marinara*
- *1 bag shredded mozzarella cheese*
- *Toppings of your choice (optional)*

Place biscuits in a deep pan side by side until the bottom of the pan is covered. Add desired amount of sauce on top of the biscuits. Bake the pizza by the directions on the biscuit can until dough is crisp.

Homemade Garlic Bread

Taste like garlic cheese sticks to me.

Ingredients:
- *6 pieces of sliced bread*
- *2 tablespoons butter*
- *⅛ teaspoon Garlic powder*
- *Shredded cheese (optional)*

Preheat oven to 400F. Lay bread on a cookie sheet.

Melt butter in microwave in 30 second intervals until melted. Add garlic powder to the melted butter and stir. Using a spoon, cover each slice of bread with butter/garlic mixture. Sprinkle shredded cheese across the top with desired amount. Bake for 15-25 minutes.

Butter Gravy

Great on biscuits or mashed potatoes.
Ingredients:
- *4 Tbsp Salted Butter (1 stick)*
- *¼ cup flour*
- *4 cups milk*
- *Black pepper (optional)*

Melt butter in a pan on medium-high heat. When butter is melted, add flour and whisk rapidly with wire whisk. Continue whisking until flour turns a light brown color, careful not to burn it. Add milk and continue whisking. As you whisk, add pepper to desired amount. Continue to whisk until gravy thickens. Turn off stove and set pan of gravy to the side to cool. Gravy will thicken as it stands.

Hardtack (1800's civil war soldier food)
For dessert, hardtack was crumbled with brown sugar and hot water. This was called "pudding". Hardtack is a versatile food that takes years to spoil as long as not exposed to moisture.
Ingredients:
- *5 cups flour*
- *1 cup water*
- *½ tablespoon of salt (optional)*

Mix flour with water that was pre-combined with salt.
Knead dough until well mixed.
Flatten int ⅜" thickness.
Cut into approximately 3-inch squares and stab with a fork several times per piece.
Bake at 400F for 30 minutes or until slightly brown.

Frugal Asian style cuisine (serves 1)
Asian food isn't like what is served in Chinese restaurants. Asian diets are typically very healthy and they eat large amounts of vegetables and rice.
Ingredients:
- *¼ cup of rice*
- *2 cups (Veggie of your choice)*
- *1 teaspoon soy sauce (optional)*

Cook rice as normal. Steam veggies.
Serve with soy sauce.

Switchel (beverage/energy drink)
Used in the 1700's as a form of an energy drink.
Switchel is both good for you and provides you with
energy on a hot summer's day.
A southern traditional drink that originated in the
Caribbeans.
Ingredients:
- *Half gallon of water*
- *½ cup of honey or molasses or sugar*
- *¼ cup Apple cider vinegar*
- *½ tablespoon of ginger powder*

Stir for at least a minute. Stir well.

Meal Ideas

Breakfast Ideas

- *Oatmeal and a banana*
- *Egg and toast*
- *Toast with Jelly*

All with a coffee or tea.

Lunch Ideas

- *PB&J w/ celery sticks or baby carrots*
- *Leftovers from the night before*
- *Cheese, nuts, apples, and cracker plate*
- *A piece of fruit or a can of fruit (in water or it's own juice, no syrups)*
- *A handful of Nuts or Trail mix*
- *Peanut butter/cheese w/ crackers*

Dinner Ideas

- *Rice and veggies w/ soy sauce (low sodium)*
- *Red beans and rice*
- *Cheese toast with homemade soup*
- *White beans (canned) with cornbread (homemade) and sliced tomato*
- *Pinto beans with cornbread and spinach*
- *Pasta with any desired sauce (alfredo, marinara, etc.) with homemade garlic bread and salad.*
- *A meat (your choice), A veggie (your choice), A carb (your choice)*

Dessert Ideas
- *Chocolate chips (serving size)*
- *Canned fruit*
- *A piece of fruit (apple, banana, etc.)*
- *A cookie*

Beverages
- *Coffee*
- *Tea*
- *Water*
- *Milk*
- *Switchel*

**Tip: Rinse your canned goods like beans and vegetables to remove a large amount of the sodium*

Save Money on Hygiene

Shower without soap
You heard me right. Soap strips the body of it's natural oils, drying out your skin and lathering you with chemicals. While soap does kill the harmful bacteria on your skin, it also kills the good bacteria as well.
You can shower with only water and nobody will be able to tell that you don't use soap, because the water rinses away the bacteria naturally; leaving some of your natural oil still on the skin.
If you have long hair, you can still wash your hair with soap, as not using soap on your hair can get rather oily and uncomfortable.

I've been showering without soap for the past year, and nobody can tell that I've not used soap. The reason I started showering without soap is because my skin is sensitive to the chemicals, and I would break out in rashes that would sting and burn. To my surprise after not using soap, I didn't stink at all. I didn't feel clean in the beginning, but after awhile it felt natural. Water alone washes the odor causing bacteria away, it seems.
The beauty in not using soap is that you no longer have to worry about keeping up with it when traveling. There's nothing to buy before going to a motel, just hop in the shower, rub your skin with water and hop out: done.

Shower every 2-3 days

Daily showers, even without soap, is even worse for your skin than using actual soap. Try to limit your showers only to every two or three days. You'll save water, time, and money.

Shower but don't take baths

Baths are a huge waste of water and you could long since be out of the shower and clean by the time you finish filling up the tub. Yes, baths are nice. They are not practical however, and cost a lot of money. You don't use as much water as you think you do when showering, and as long as you keep your shower under 5 minutes, you can save a ton of money.

Sure, some might argue to just fill with an inch of water and use that. I've tried that, and to be completely honest, you don't get all the soap off your skin or get as clean as you do with a shower. That's just an opinion though.

Shave with soap

You can use any type of soap for this, though personally I use bar soap. Wet your skin before hand, and then wet the bar of soap. Lather up the soap in your hands and apply it to the area you wish to shave. Next, wet your hand with water and rub over the lathered soap on your skin to make it really slick. Shave as normal.

No shaving cream required! Plus, you can use the soap for other purposes as well, like washing your hands: unlike shaving cream.

Re-sharpen/Clean your disposable razors

A razor has multiple uses to the frugal, and shaving is one of them. Forget using them one time and then tossing them in the trash. That's a waste!

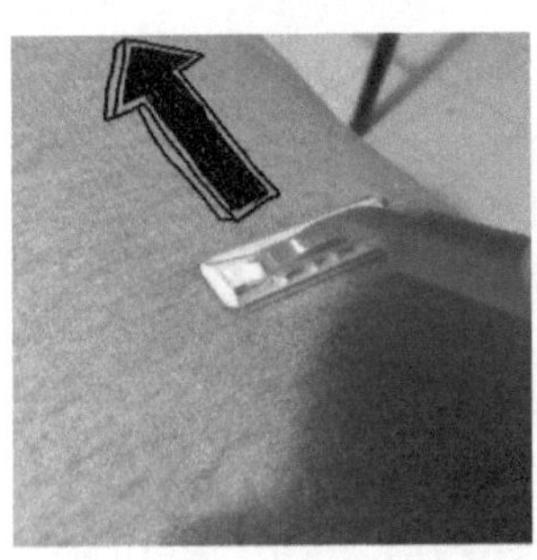

I've re-used the same disposable razor for months using a re-sharpening technique I found on the internet. Simply take a pair of denim jeans, press the face of the down onto the denim with firm pressure, and push forward. You do this in short strokes, picking the head of the razor off the denim, setting it back to it's starting location, and pushing forward. Like a stropping motion.

You repeat this until the razor is re-sharpened, usually about 10-15 times, always pushing forward. If you pull the razor towards you during this process, you'll cut your denim.

To clean the dead skin and oil build up from your razor, soak the head of it in a cup with rubbing alcohol. Let the head of the razor soak in the alcohol for about 10-20 minutes. Rinse with water. *Use a Q-tip/Toothpick to clean hair off the razor blades, never your finger.*

Stop buying toilet paper

People of olden times used everything from crumpled newspapers, washcloths, leaves, dirt, and even just under running water. You decide what's best, but I'm telling you that buying something with the sole intention of throwing it away afterwards is a complete waste of money.
Unless you don't have to pay for it, then use it!

Cut your own hair
You can have a friend do it, or you can do it yourself. There's no reason to be high-maintenance and needing to go to a hair salon once a week. Personally, I shave my head. I don't worry about style, I don't give a flying fig newton about fashion: I'm saving money by doing it myself.
If long hair is too much of a hassle then do what I did and cut your hair off.
If you don't want to cut your hair off, simply let it grow and don't bother styling it or just style it at home with a friend.

You might be thinking, but I'm a woman? So? Who said because of your gender that you had to have long hair? Your beauty is much deeper than just what is on the surface. A woman with short hair gives off a sense of strength and power. There's nothing wrong with being you and proud of it!

Share unscented deodorant with your spouse
This might sound gross, but not having a scent to the deodorant allows you both to use one single type and not one particular smell or scent due to

gender. It saves you money to only buy one for the both of you rather than one each.

Skimp on Deodorant
Only do this if you're at home and have nowhere to go. As long as you don't offend anyone, skimping on deodorant is okay!
Please, for the love of all that is holy, wear deodorant if you're going in public!

Clean your toothbrush with boiling water
I've hear that you need to replace your toothbrush at least once a month. Who said? Why? Apparently because of bacteria came the response. Disinfect it by bringing water to a rolling boil and then pour hot water over the head of the toothbrush, being careful not to pour it on yourself. Use common sense and don't get too close: steam can burn you. (Can't believe I have to say this)

Brush your teeth with baking soda
Many people don't like the fluoride that is put in our toothpaste. I was also one of those people. I discovered that instead of paying high dollar for toothpaste that had no fluoride, why not use the classic baking soda method? Simply apply a little of the baking soda to your toothbrush, add a drop of water, and brush like you normally would. Some people add peroxide to the baking soda for disinfecting and whitening purposes.

Frugal Hygiene Shopping List

- *Toothbrush*
- *Bar soap (your choice)*
- *Baking Soda (for brushing your teeth)*
- *Disposable Razors*
- *Unscented Deodorant (or your choice)*
- *Cotton swabs (for your ears)*
- *Feminine products (if applicable)*
- *Shampoo and Conditioner (if long hair applies)*
- *Emery board*
- *Hair clipper set*

Save Money on Cleaning Supplies

Make your own
You don't even have to buy a large majority of household cleaners. You can make a lot of your cleaning supplies at home, often without the use of harmful chemicals that are hard on the lungs.

Laundry Detergent
½ part Borax
½ part Washing Soda
Optional: (Add a few essential oil drops for scents)
Mix both ingredients into a container. Use between 1-2 tablespoons and ¼ of a cup depending on the size of your laundry load

Laundry Detergent and Fabric Softener
½ cup of Distilled Vinegar to your wash load
(Detergent)
1 cup of Distilled Vinegar to the last rinse cycle
(Fabric Softener)

Dryer Sheets
(helps remove static cling)
- *Add ½ of a cup of Baking Soda to your wash.*
- *Dampen a washcloth with Distilled Vinegar*
- *Two balls of rolled aluminum foil*

Glass Cleaner
1 part Distilled Vinegar

7 parts water
Spray onto surface, wipe clean with microfiber cloth.

Multi-Surface Cleaner
1 cup Distilled Vinegar
1 cup Water
1 Teaspoon of Baking Soda
Spray bottle
(A few drops of essential oil for scent is optional)
Combine vinegar, water, and baking soda in a spray bottle.
**Vinegar is said to cut grease and disinfect surfaces: killing E.coli and Salmonella as well as other "gram negative" bacteria. However, it does not kill staphylococcus.*

Wood Polish

1 Tablespoon Olive oil
1 Teaspoon Distilled Vinegar
⅛ Teaspoon of Lemon Juice
Combine into a small jar or container. Apply only a little of the mixture to a cloth. Rub on surface, going with the grain. Rub the mixture into the wood.

Brass Polish

Sponge
Lemon Juice
Salt
Dampen the sponge with lemon juice, sprinkle salt on top of the sponge. Apply to brass.

Brass Cleaner

½ cup Distilled Vinegar
1 teaspoon Salt
Flour
Dissolve salt into vinegar in a container. Gradually add flour until vinegar mixture becomes a paste. Rub into the brass and let stand 10-12 minutes. Rinse with warm water.
Buff dry.

Disinfectant
1 part Rubbing Alcohol
1 part Water
Spray Bottle

Combine water and rubbing alcohol into a spray bottle. Shake lightly for a few seconds.
To use, spray close onto the surface area. Wait a few seconds, wipe clean with cloth.
**Alternatively, you can soak children's toys with hydrogen peroxide/water solution to disinfect them. Rinse them afterwards.*

Drain Cleaner
1 cup baking soda
1 cup vinegar
Pot of boiling water

Dump baking soda down the drain, pour in vinegar. Wait 10 minutes, dump boiling water down the drain, check results. (Plungers may help unclog the pipe)

Shoe shiner
1 squirt of Hand Lotion

Dab some hand lotion onto your desired shoe. Work in the lotion and then buff with rag.

Ink/Permanent marker stain remover
-Rubbing Alcohol

Pour rubbing alcohol over ink/permanent marker stain, wipe with rag.

Weed Killer

2 cups Distilled vinegar
Pour vinegar onto the desired weed/grass you want to kill.

Floor Cleaner

Baking soda
Distilled white vinegar
Bucket ½ full of warm water
Measurements may differ depending on size of bucket, but assuming you're using a small 1 gallon bucket, pour ½ cup of vinegar and ½ tablespoon of baking soda into the bucket. Be sure to have the bucket in your bathtub in case of overflow.
This cleaner is great for most floors to my knowledge I use it on my hardwood floor and linoleum without any problems.

Alternative:
Borax
Warm water
In a 1 gallon bucket, add ½ cup of borax to a ½ full bucket of warm water.
A great multipurpose floor cleaner.

General Tips:
- Label your cleaners in their containers with permanent markers.
- ½ cup Baking soda can be added to super smelly laundry for both as a degreaser and odor eliminator.
- Make only enough for 1-3 months use. Replace after 3 months as they have lower shelf lives due to not being filled with unnatural chemicals.

(Though I've had homemade window cleaner for a year and it still works)
- Hydrogen Peroxide is a natural occuring bleach and is a disinfectant. Clean door knobs and other surfaces by applying peroxide to a cloth and then wiping clean.

- **Don't mix vinegar and baking soda into a bottle and seal it. The pressure can cause the container to rupture in your hand.**

- **Coffee filters can be used as window rags**

Save Money on Clothing

Where to buy clothing?
Second Hand stores, thrift shops, Salvation Armies, Goodwills, used clothing stores, or closet clothing stores.
You could search the internet for used clothing in bulk, as people moving are constantly trying to shed the weight of extra items. Some might give it away free.

How to get free clothing?
Ask for clothing as gifts during the holidays.
Search the internet for free clothing.
Dumpster diving. (Believe it or not, I've a lot of clothing this way.) However, there are risks that come with diving into a dumpster, so not the best way to get free clothing; It's also not guaranteed.

When to buy clothes?
Only buy clothes when you absolutely need them (either for work or a special occasion) and when you do buy them, never buy them new.
You'll rarely ever encounter the situation where you absolutely **MUST** buy new clothes. A large majority of your clothing bought is done so on a whim. Try to control yourself when you're out shopping and see clearance clothing.
Remember that unless it's $3.00 or less each, it's not a good deal.

You can buy some seriously expensive and nice clothes from a secondhand store for a little under $3.00 usually. Some of them are even name brand! If your weight has changed, either via pregnancy or otherwise, that is the time to consider buying comfortable clothing. If your clothing is too tight or way oversized, that is another time to consider buying different clothing.

"Wear your clothes to the point they fall apart in the washer."

The only other time to buy new clothes beyond that point is if your old clothing is so worn out it is falling apart beyond repair, or there is a special occasion and you do not already have the appropriate attire. Ex. (Funerals, weddings, formalities, etc.) Even then, try to obtain those clothes used rather than actually buying them new. For instance, you could potentially find a name brand polo for around $1.50 and save money from what would have been easily $5.00 or greater. You could ask for socks or clothing for the holidays.

Why buy used?
We live in a society where the "new and improved" is associated with the cool crowd and is considered fashionable. We all have it instilled in us that wearing clothing that was worn by somebody else somehow makes us less important. Suddenly by wearing used clothing, that we become "trash".

F**k what anybody thinks about you; be yourself
and be proud.
There isn't anything wrong with buying used
"anything". We live in a culture where we're taught
from a young age to abolish the old and stick with
the new. It's left us all in a state of discontentment
to be completely honest.
Our western culture wastes so many things that it is
in fact the smarter option to buy used, simply to
help clear up waste in the local dump.
If it still is wearable, wear it. That's the motto.

How long to keep my clothes?
A large majority of your clothes will last for years
and years to come, most of the time not needing
repairs. You should only replace your clothes when
the ones you have are lost, worn out to the point of
being unwearable, or your weight has changed.
At that point, donate the clothing back to the
second hand store for someone else to use.
From this point forward, do not buy anymore
unneeded clothing if you wish to save money.

What type of clothing to buy?
Jackets, dresses, work pants, blue jeans, shorts,
khakis, slacks, polos, shirts with either long sleeves
or short ones, muscle shirts, and nearly anything
else that isn't underwear--- buy it used.

What about Underwear?

Never buy used underwear of any kind. This includes: Lingerie, bras, panties, briefs, boxers, boxer-briefs, socks, or tank tops/undershirts.
If it fits in this category---- buy it new, always of a generic brand.

What about belts and accessories?
Buy them new if it goes into the body like a piercing. Anything external like a necklace or a bracelet can be either used or new as long as it isn't expensive.
As long as they are affordable, buy belts new. People prefer different sizes, materials, and need different types for different occasions--- so buy them new.
Webbed belts are currently the cheapest.

Shoes?

Shoes are like underwear: you don't want to catch something from somebody who wore it before you, therefore buy it new.

Personally contracted athlete's foot once from wearing used shoes, even after washing them. Generic shoes are sometimes just as durable as name brand, and sometimes cost up to 90% less.

Some people would argue that name brand is better because you could wear the same pair for years.

I argue that I've worn the same pair of generic shoes for years. Personal preferences aside, I was the one who paid less for my shoes.

You should own no more than four pairs of shoes.

One pair of each in one of the four categories:

- **Athletic:** For running and exercising; yard chores.
- **Dress:** For job interviews, formal occasions.
- **Boots:** Steel toe work boots are best; they are for the dangerous jobs like factory work and moving furniture where you might injure your toes.
- **House shoes:** Slippers, flip flops, whatever you wear in the house.

Kids clothing

Kids outgrow their clothes at a rapid rate so it only makes complete senses to buy them used clothing. Follow the same rules you would for yourself.
Outerwear, Jackets, shirts, pants, and dresses---Used.
Underwear---New and generic.
Shoes---New and generic.

Backpacks?

Buy them used if you can find what you need for an affordable price-- otherwise buy used and generic.

Save Money on Utilities/Doing without

Electricity usage

Keep the lights off at day and open the curtains/blinds and let some daylight in. Not only is sunlight a great mood booster, but it's also free light!

Replace the classic incandescent light bulbs that use ridiculous amounts of energy for the lowest  powered economy bulb you can find. Economy bulbs are pricey, but one bulb is said to last years. They produce the same amount of lighting, but use ridiculously less watts than the incandescent. I've save tons of money just by using economy bulbs. Use only one bulb per outlet regardless of how many bulb outlets are in the room. One economy bulb per room only.

Shut off that television you're using for background noise, and anything not in use.

Shut off and unplug unused appliances, and depending on the weather and season, open a window and let some fresh air in.

Turn your refrigerator settings to 38 F and your freezer to 8 F if applicable. This will make your refrigerator work less and use less power to maintain it's inside temperature.

Turn down your water heater's temperature to 120F
or less. (Some have alphabetical settings, you'll
have to research what temperature they mean as it
could vary depending on the model.)
Insulate the water pipes on the water heater using
a special tape made for it to help save money in
that regard. A lot of money gets wasted on
electricity just by the water heater.

Seasonal electric savings
Insulate your roof with extra insulation first and
foremost regardless of the season.
In the spring and summer, set the thermostat to no
less than 68 F; or turn it off and open the windows.
Set a box fan in the window blowing inward to help
pull cool air from the outside into your house.

In the fall and winter, set the thermostat to 68 F.
Wear extra layers around the house, and cover the
windows with weatherize window kits or plastic
sheeting. It's like adding extra glass to the window
as it further insulates it and prevents cold drafts
from sapping your home's heat.
Put weather stripping around the doors to keep
your heating and cooling costs down.
Use heavy curtains on the windows to further
insulate them from the cold.

Water usage savings

Avoid baths. Shower every single time. You'll save money and be out of the shower long before the tub finished filling up. Try to shower as quickly as possible so that you don't waste water. You'll save money that way.

Don't flush every single time you urinate in the toilet. Yes, it will stain the bowl if you don't clean the bowl once a week. Don't let the urine stagnate all day or it will stink. If you live in a household with multiple people and one bathroom, their likely going to flush it shortly after you so save money by flushing every other time you urinate.

Defecating on the other hand, flush every single time.

(If you're not comfortable with this recommendation, you don't have to follow it)

Make sure that none of your faucets are leaking; every drop adds up.

If your monthly water bill seems abnormally high, be sure and check the pipes underneath the basement/crawlspace of your home for leaks.

Do laundry by hand

You can take a small bucket or bathtub and fill it half way with warm water. Add ½ cup of homemade laundry detergent and wash by scrubbing the clothing together with your knuckles and repeatedly wringing it out. Rinse it under the faucet, then wring it tightly. Hang up to air dry either indoors or out.

Internet and Cellphones

The internet is great, cellphones are too. The problem being is that their services are way overpriced.

Dial up is still the cheapest internet option out there, and can be found by searching for it on a search engine.

Get both the cheapest plans available to you for internet and cell phone, and be sure to ask if there is a data limit on your internet.

With cheap phone plans there are little data limits, sure. No unlimited data is only a problem if you use your phone a majority of the time away from the house. When at home you're already paying for Wi-Fi so just use the "unlimited data" you have at home on your smartphone as well.

There's no need to stay connected constantly anyway. You have unlimited talk and text with the cheapest phone plan, use it.

Some kids out here these days will stand in the middle of the mall and snap a picture of themselves.

When I was their age I actually looked at the products in the mall rather than look at myself on a screen. I can do that with a mirror at home, why do it in public?

Phones

Landlines seem to be more expensive than cell phones these days, but do offer a few advantages over the cell phone. For instance, if you were on an apartment floor and called from a cell phone to emergency services, they would have your GPS location but not know what floor you were on. With a landline, the phone number is already tied to your address so the 911 operator can get emergency services to you even if you fail to provide the address.

It's cell or landline. Pick one depending on your preference. Some folks pick landline because they don't like being available constantly. With those folks, I would agree 100%.

Insurance

Auto insurance is mandatory by law, and we already know that we have no control of the price nor how it fluctuates. If you don't have a vehicle then you're already a step ahead (pun intended) of the game. You don't have to worry about gas and vehicle expenses. You don't worry about having a place to park.

One insurance I would suggest to you is renter's insurance. That way if your house/apartment burns down, or your items get stolen, you'll be able to replace everything. Plus, bundling renters insurance with auto supposedly lowers your rates. (Don't quote me on that)

Doing without

If you have a monthly fee that isn't Insurance/Electricity/Water/Garbage related, you can choose to let it go. This is called doing without, and it will be what saves you money in the long run. For instance, I don't *need* a monthly subscription for a phone app I don't hardly use.
Cell phones and Internet can be done without as well. A phone is still important to have, whether a landline or cell phone, as you need one in emergencies.
Internet isn't required unless you work from home. If you want the absolute cheapest option, you could get dial up internet.

Save Money on Shelter

Cheaper to rent?
Renting provides you often with free maintenance, but the short answer to this question is no. Renting does not give you the financial security that owning your own home does. Nor does it help you with getting loans. You can also sell your home if you choose to relocate, making it easier to move. Another reason it's better to own is because you can leverage your house for money.

Mobile homes
Mobile homes are unlike houses in multiple ways. They tend to be cheaper to buy, unlike houses. Initially this seems to be an advantage, but unfortunately mobile homes depreciate with time instead of gain value.
(Whatever sense that makes, it's still property)

There's also a stigma that comes about people who live in mobile homes but the reality of those people is that they are down to earth people just trying to make it by. A large majority of them being working class people.
Sure, not everybody is good company that lives in a mobile home, but that can be said for a large majority of people on the planet regardless of where they live.

Vehicle living

In the fall of 2016 I spent nearly a year and a half living in my car. I weathered the winter nights and the intense summer days all in the comfort of my old 2008 Jeep Patriot.
Many people these days have the same idea and seem to be ditching a large majority of their possessions and moving into their vehicles.
The benefits of this become suddenly apparent. You can move anywhere, and live anywhere. Nothing no longer holds you back except your lack of income. You'll still have to work a job or save up enough to relocate.

You no longer have to pay anything but car maintenance, insurance, gas, and car payments (if any).
The downside is that if you have a family or someone in the car with you, things get cramped real fast. My wife and I were arguing over everything from where to sleep to where we should place the box of food.

Your diet will go to crap too, but this isn't always the case as long as you stay away from tempting options like fast food.
The weather will make it challenging to live in your vehicle if you live in an area with intense summer heat or cold nights.
Then, there's the constant threat of crime from individuals around you. My advice is to park in a 24hr supermarket parking lot for the night. I've slept there time and time again. Living in your car is a

challenge that is both exciting and allows you to
see the world, so long as your income holds out.

Sure, you could work from your vehicle too. I did
that for several months. I bought a gym
membership and showered for one monthly
payment and often exercised there to pass the time
that I wasn't working or sleeping.
Libraries proved to be another place to hang out
while I was waiting to go to work, as it had free
internet and computers to use.
Parks were a place to workout or just get out of the
car. I kept instant coffee in my car and got free hot
water from fast food joints for morning coffee.
It's certainly a thrilling experience and I'd gladly do
it all over again.

Apartments
Apartments are great for those just starting out in
the world. If you want my personal advice, stay
away from the overly cheap ones as the riff-raff
tend to flock to it. You'll likely encounter roaches,
bad neighbors, or from my own personal
experience: a convicted sex offender on one side of
me and drug dealers in the apartment on the other
side that blasted their music and smoked weed on
the balcony. What was worse, the landlady was a
pushover: never enforcing the rules.
Your experience may vary.
Not worth $450.00/monthly with paid utilities.

If you're looking for an apartment, try to find one that is $550 or more a month for rent. That helps keep the unruly neighbors away.

I know this guide is supposed to be about frugality, but sometimes your sanity (and safety) is more important.

Squatting

If you wanted to get by without any money at all, you could potentially find a large area of woodland and set up a hidden shelter and live out of it. I've often toyed with the idea myself, though if you get caught you could deal with legal consequences and potential jail time.

Probably not a good idea to try, but it's there.

Save money on Furniture

Buy your curtains without rods
This was a mistake I made one too many times. I'd
go to the store when I would move to a new place,
and the first thing I'd buy is curtains and curtain
rods.
I'd pay $3.50 per rod per window. Later I
discovered that all I had to do was take a staple
gun and staple the curtains above the window. No
visitors have ever noticed it. (or even mentioned it)
You could also use thumbtacks, though this makes
it kind of obvious that you're doing so. Still, if you
don't mind what visitors might say, do it anyway.

Get it free
Look on the internet classifieds for free furniture or
dig it out of the trash.
I personally steer clear of this so as to not contract
roaches or bed bugs.

Buy basic furniture/Don't rent it
Pay outright for your furniture rather than rent it
from a rental store. This should be common sense
as you pay nearly twice as much for the furniture
than what you would pay just buying it outright.
Sure, I get it that you want it now.
Sometimes though, it's better to wait for things.

Basic furniture for each room

Living room
-Coffee table
-Floor rug
-Pillows to sit on the floor
-Bookshelf
-A place to set a small TV (small table, etc)
-Television (19" or less if you want it)
-TV Antenna

Kitchen
-Simple table
-Folding chairs
-Small portable fridge
-Portable corded burner for cooking
-Toaster oven for baking
-Coffee pot

Bedroom
-Foam floor mats or camping cot or air mattress
-Pillows/blankets
-A container to store your clothes

Laundry
-A place to wash clothes (bathtub, bucket, etc.)
-Clothesline
-Hangers or clothespins
(Hand washing clothing, hanging it up to dry)

Save money on Home Security

Single shot shotgun

Source:https://tpwd.texas.gov/education/hunter-education/online-course/firearms-and-ammunition-1/shotguns

A single shot break-barrel shotgun is one of the most affordable guns that one can own. You can pick one up at a local pawn shop or gun store from anywhere around $50-$150 depending on the model. Even if you just ask around, sometimes somebody will have an old break-barrel shotgun laying about they'd be willing to give you. Single shots require little practice to learn how to operate, and their loading and unloading mechanisms make them safer for those inexperienced with firearms.

Gauges

They come in several common gauges from heaviest load and hardest recoil to lightest:

- *10 Gauge (+70 lbs recoil, hardest recoiling modern shotgun)*
- *12 Gauge (Middle-ground of shotguns, recoil varies and can be light or heavy depending on load, most common gauge of shotgun.)*

- *16 Gauge (Not as common but still widely used.)*
- *20 Gauge (Second most common gauge of shotgun due to availability. Has a much lighter recoil than the 12 gauge and is great as a home-defense weapon for the elderly or people who are recoil sensitive.)*
- *.410 Gauge (Third most common shotgun, by far the smallest of the shotguns family. It's recoil is light, and it's an affordable choice for those who don't like recoil or young shooters.)*

There are other gauges out there, but these are currently the most common as of the year 2019.

Shotgun Adapters

What makes these guns so versatile is the fact that the break barrel shotgun can receive adapters which allow them to shoot other types of ammo. You can find adapters that allow it to shoot .22LR, .45, .357, 9mm, etc. Essentially turning your shotgun into a smoothbore rifle. The added bonus to the versatility is the fact that it's a shotgun. As you may know, a 12 gauge shotgun can be used to take nearly every single animal on the planet due to its versatile ammo types.

Shotgun ammunition

There are three easily available commercial rounds for the shotgun:

- Slugs: One large projectile. Gives your shotgun more range and is devastating to whatever it hits; designed for large game and as defense rounds. Some are rifled which means they can be shot in a standard smoothbore without a special barrel, and some slugs require a special barrel. For most single shot smoothbores, rifled slugs are best.

(Don't shoot slugs out of a full-choke shotgun.)

- Buckshot: Generally the size of a pea or smaller. Buckshot has the effective spread of birdshot for quick moving targets, but with the killing capabilities of deer and large game. They are listed as 00 and 000 which are pronounced double-aught (00) and triple-aught (000).

- Birdshot: Very small shot. Meant for small game and birds. Designed especially for hitting fast moving targets.
Can range in shot sizes from greatest to least: #4-#12
For home security, bird shot isn't recommended, but if it's all you have, use it. It's better than nothing at all.

Hunting and Home security
You could use your shotgun for hunting as well as home security. It can put meat on the table and save you money in the bank.

For home security purposes, you might feel that it is lacking in ammo capacity, but the reality of this situation is that generally bad guys flee after the first shot is fired. Generally only in home invasions; not in other scenarios. Still, with practice you'll be able to get off many shots in under a single minute. A single-shot shotgun is better than being barehanded.

Plus if you ever find yourself down on your luck or needing quick cash, you could just as well sell your shotgun and then buy another later.

Gun ownership is a proud American tradition, and should be a right to every citizen the world over. Sadly, most other countries don't allow firearms to its citizens. Therefore, I've included a non-firearm section.

Non-Gun Security*

#1. Buy a can of pepper spray and learn how to use it. Don't spray it in enclosed areas, and if you do, get to fresh air or out of the room ASAP.

#2. Most people buy a baseball bat (or in other countries a cricket bat) usually of the smaller variety. It doubles as a way to play sports, or you could take your frustrations out on an inanimate object.

Anything with weight and is solid can be used as a weapon. Heavy, metal flashlights are another option.

You can pick up a sporting bat nearly everywhere. Pawn shops, yard sales, secondhand malls, on the internet, or even free.

#3. I've heard of people using archery equipment for home security, such as crossbows, pistol crossbows, and regular bows. I've even heard stories of people using Co2 Pistols and pellet rifles to ward off home intruders.

I guess any ranged weapon is better than nothing, they say.

Even if you have a weapon:

Get to a room with a lockable door, lock door, hide, call the police.

(These are just ideas, I the author am not responsible for the situational outcome, financial loss, any injury, loss of life, property damage, or any crimes committed.)

2x4 Door Bar

You'll need:

- *An 8ft 2x4*
- *2 zinc bar holders*
- *3" (or 3 ½ ") #10 or greater Screws*
- *A hand drill and the respective bit for the screws*

Door Bar Placement

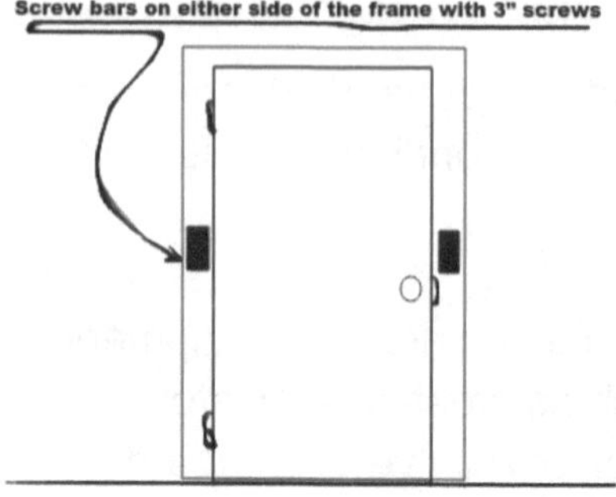

Is a method in which you'll fasten (2) zinc bar holders on either side of the door frame leveled across from each other. They will then be secured to the inner wall studs of the frame by 3" screws which you'll drill in place. Afterwards, simply cut to length a section of 2x4 that is the width span between the zinc bar holders so that each end of the board overhangs either side of the bar holders.

Heavily resistant to kick-ins. Make sure the board sits against the door.

Door Bar Placement

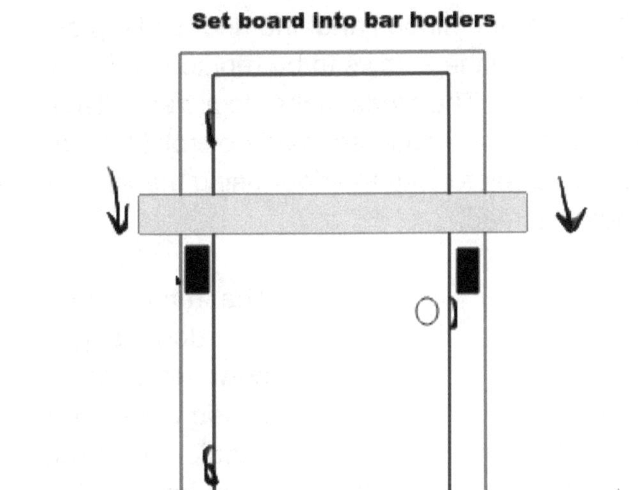

Door Reinforcement

The main weak points in door entryways lie in where the door makes contact with the frame. These are the hinges and the door strike plate; both require the screws to be replaced with three-inch screws. The studs of the door frame itself that is a part of the house are made of solid lumber: therefore reinforcing the door using the frame of the house instead.

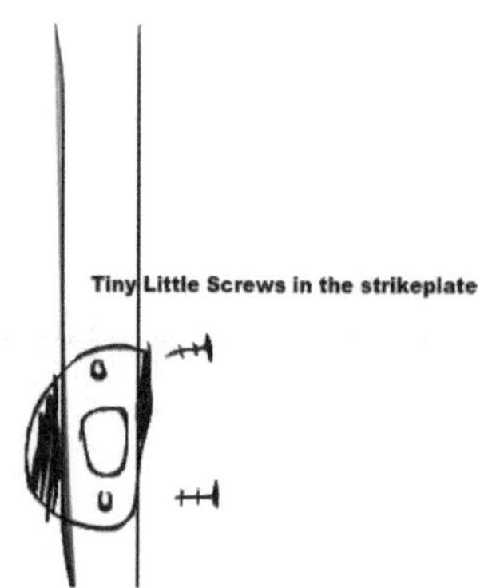

The frame from which your door hangs however is made of cheap wood, and should not be relied upon for security as they are known to shatter under brute force.

-    **Remove screws from the hinges one at a time while replacing each removed small screw with a large #10 3" Screw.**
Adding extra hinges further increases strength and durability of the door being seated onto the frame.

-    **Remove the small screws from the strike plate. (where the door latch makes contact with the frame; that peculiar piece of metal you may or may not**

already know about) Replace the small screws with #10 3" screws.

This extra reinforcement will further increase your door's stability during an attempted invasion, which will decrease their chances of breaking in your door. At the very least, it will prevent them from kicking it down within 10 seconds.

Door Guard Plates

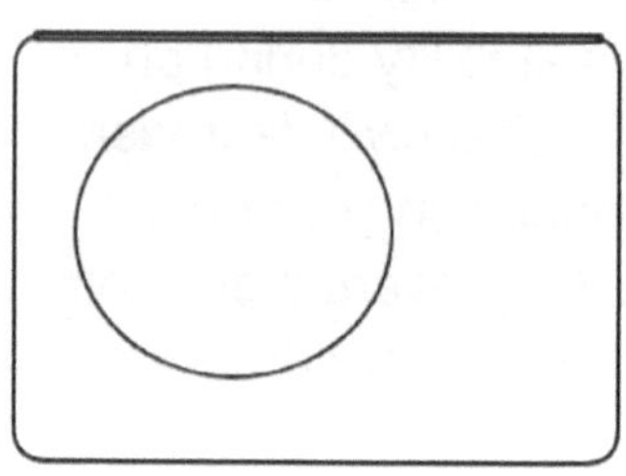

Door Guard Plate

Door Guard Plates are steel plates that reinforce where the door knob and deadbolt sit inside of the door. This are near the latch is known to shatter under force causing the latch to give way and the door knob to fail.

Adding a door guard plate reinforces this area and allows the door to withstand more force.

Plates can be found online or at your local hardware store and generally expensive compared to simply barring the door. However, Guard plates used in conjunction with extra door hinges and reinforced strike plates for both the deadbolt and the knob will provide a great deal of durability to an assault on your door. You may choose to go this route for the sake of aesthetics; yet the door isn't entirely pry proof or kick resistant as a door bar would provide. Guard plates are an option that can be used alongside door bars and other reinforcements for an extra layer of security or for when you're away and not able to bar the door.

2x4 Wedge

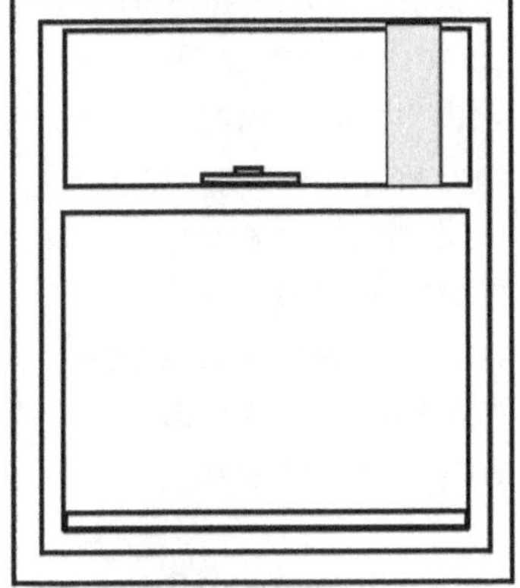

Window Jambs

Functioning much like the Glass sliding door counter part or the back door wood, the 2x4 window wedge is simply lodging a piece of lumber or wooden dowel between the moving window and the frame itself: preventing it from being opened.

To make the wedge, measure the space between the window from the frame to the top of the moving panel. Cut the board/dowel to fit and make sure it fits tight enough to prevent falling out yet is easy to remove.

Porch lights and Door alarms

Not wanting to invest extra money into motion lights and fancy gizmos? Simply turn on your porch light every night. It serves as both a deterrent and a means of illumination. It's best used in conjunction with energy saving bulbs and will have to be switched off every morning; but you're working with what you have and that's the smart way to look at it.

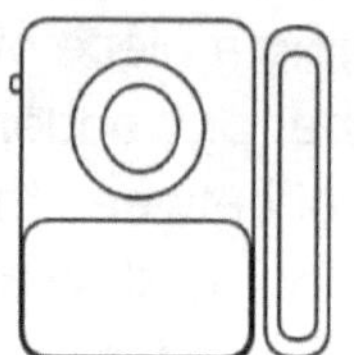

A great deterrent to home invasions are 120 decibel door alarms that when used in conjunction with "Security system on premises" stickers strikes fear in home intruders.

They are quite affordable and extremely loud. Sure to alert you to your door being opened, and sending the home intruder fleeing into the night.

Window safety tips

- Keep your windows covered with either a thick bed sheet, a curtain, or blinds to prevent nosy creepers and potential intruders from spying on you and your family.

- Anti-break film is a great extra layer for your home's security as windows are the second method to which home intruders gain entry to your home. Combined with a vibration window alarm, your windows will be as nearly as impenetrable as you could possibly make them.

    (y'know aside from actually
    boarding the windows up…)

- Do not leave your blinds/curtains/sheets open at night or when you're gone as people can see in and spy on both your family and probe your possessions.

- Always check the windows before you leave if you live in a house with other people. The reason being is that you never know when a window was opened last and so it is better to just check and be on the safe side.

- Do not seal windows as a form of home security. Windows can be used as emergency exits and should therefore be as accessible as possible.

The Mighty Pupper

When you think of buying a dog for home security purposes, you naturally want the biggest and baddest breed known to man. You want a rottweiler, or a doberman or maybe a german shepherd. Realistically, the size of the dog or the breed doesn't determine it's fight. I've personally known pitbulls that were big babies that wouldn't hurt a fly, and then had poodles that would tear my fingers all to hell with their teeth just for trying to pet them.

It boils down to most of the more vicious dogs being breeds like the jack russell and chihuahua. These dogs won't strike fear into the hearts of home intruders, but they can be vicious as all hell and make a lot of noise. Good luck getting a chihuahua to stop growling and barking. Maybe they are inherently born with "little dog syndrome" and that's why they try to compensate by being so fierce. Whatever the case, little dogs are the best way to go.

Don't buy a dog and put it on a chain outside all by itself for the rest of its life all in the name of security. Nah, if you want serious protection then get a small indoor dog.
Take note than having a small dog is still a pet, and so therefore you will have vet bills and have to provide it with food and water. Dogs also provide the benefit of companionship and love and should

be bought for these reasons over security purposes as they are living beings worthy of love just like the rest of us.

Chances are if the dog you have bonds with you, it will also protect you: regardless of breed. Small dogs are easier to care for, but you shouldn't overlook larger dogs either.

Choose whatever dog you prefer. That's your personal taste.

Give me A Sign

Even if you don't own a dog, putting up a cheap "Beware of Dog" sign from your local hardware store will work as a deterrent in and of itself. If you do have a dog, then having this sign in a visible location likely prevents the intruder from suing you if he gets bitten after breaking in (stupid isn't it?) and possibly injured or killed by your dog.

A shame we live in a society where criminals can sue you just for you defending yourself in your own home. If you live in a state where you have "castle doctrine" then you likely don't have anything to worry about.

Having both "Home security system" and "Beware of dogs" signs are great deterrents and relatively inexpensive. You can further add to the idea that you own a dog (even if you don't) by putting a ball in your front yard and putting a food bowl on your front porch.

Remember: Dogs alone don't prevent you from becoming a target.

Ideal Safe Room

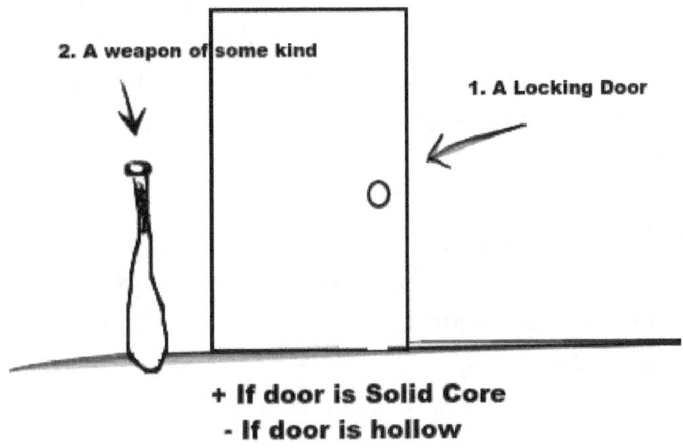

The ideal safe room will have a weapon and a lockable door. Having a backup phone in this room isn't a bad idea either.

You'll want to flee to your safe room as soon as possible and be sure to barricade the door as well if possible. You can use a 2x4 bar in this room as well. The goal is to have a location to retreat to and wait for the police to arrive.

Another good idea is to keep most of your valuables in this room as well in order to cut the burglar's losses. Having a solid core door and reinforced hinges are a good idea as well.

Save Money on Transportation

Sell extra vehicles
If you don't need it, and you don't use it then sell it. Guys go out and buy these overly expensive classic cars and fix them up. If that's your thing, by all means. I however, would trade the chains of too many possessions for a simpler and more minimalist life.

Walk or ride a bike
If wherever you're going isn't that far from your home, consider taking off on foot and leaving the old gas hog at home.
Plus, better for the environment that way and free exercise.

Clean your car and remove excess weight
Hauling around a bunch of stuff you don't use can really drain the tank. This is more for trucks than small cars and suvs, as there is likely to be debris and other items in the bed.
The rule still applies for non-trucks though: clean it out.

Calm your driving

When you gun it right after the light turns green, you're burning the hell out of your gas. Slow it down and accelerate slower. Drive the speed limit: you'll get there when you get there.

Carpooling

If you have co-workers that also need a ride, you guys could decide to share vehicles on different days or give each other rides home from work. This will save each of you a large amount of gas money in the long run which can be saved up.

Use Public transport

Buses and subways are great ways to get around but as of right now charge a toll. You'll get further for cheaper and pay less than owning a vehicle. Sadly, you'll have to share those rides with random strangers, some with possibly bad intentions.

Don't pay for a carwash

Wash your car at home if you care about that sort of thing. Avoid the carwash like the plague as they merely provide everything you could do at home, for a heftier fee.

If you don't think a five dollar bill is anything, then drop one in a jar whenever you clean your car. Use that money at the end of the month that you would've spent at the carwash on something else. See the point?

Or you could just wait for it to rain like I do.

Don't speed

Yeah, people want to get there fast. Our society is all about having things right now. We want it now, we don't wanna wait, etc.

Slow it down if you want to save gas. Wake up and smell the coffee; life isn't about having everything instantaneously. We all know "those" types of people on the road. They get mad and speed around us and then we flip them off and get upset. Yeah, those type.

The same idiot that you pull up behind at a stop light moments later. You'd think if they'd done the math that they're not getting anywhere any quicker by speeding.

If they're driving 65 mph and you're going 55 mph, there's only going to be a few minutes difference in arrival times.

(He'll only be 10 miles ahead in an hour)

Is that difference worth risking their lives and everyone around them? They seem to think so.

Save Money on Entertainment

Getting bored?
Don't sit there and mindlessly stare at moving pictures on a screen. Get up and live life! Pick up a new hobby, try new things, cook a meal or go for a walk. Do chores around the house. Exercise. Read a book. Play with your pet. Talk to friends or play a board game.

Books
Libraries are a great place to get free books to read and you can return them when your done.
If you like having a bookshelf, then buying books from thrift stores and used bookstores are a great way to amass an affordable collection.
A lot of people these days are reading their books on E-readers electronically. There's a huge market out there for electronic books and a large majority of public domain works to get free reading content. Books are great way to learn things and occupy your time.

Games
A pack of playing cards and some friends can go a long way for entertainment. Board games like chess and checkers provide tons of fun and obtaining a set is relatively cheap.

Exercise

A good hour spent doing push-ups and lifting weights is a great way to stay in shape and pass the time.
If you're not up to working out, try doing chores around the house or yard. Stay moving and accomplish things too!

Antenna TV
These days people have cable and satellite televisions, which is quickly moving up to smart TV's with all their doohickies and thingamabobs.
Most people complain about their cable bill but don't realize that there is free TV out there!
It's completely free television, all you have to do is buy a good antenna and hook it up to your television.
It's not like back in the 70's where you only had 3 channels. These days you get ten or more, often being popular stations that good shows come on.

Radio
Nothing beats the ability to kick back and listen to some music. You could be driving down the road in your car, or using a pocket radio.
Music tends to be poetry for the soul, and is a great cheap way to entertain a few hours or kill the silence.

Practice a hobby

Gardening, archery, hunting, fishing, studying wild edibles, surfing, hiking, camping, painting, knitting, drawing, cooking, learning new things, lifting weights, even shooting a rubber band gun at tin cans is something you can do!

Save Money on Healthcare

Wash your hands
If this was the only advice I could give, it would be
enough. Wash your hands after being out in public,
before eating, and after touching doorknobs. This
will save you more often than not from getting sick.
Washing those hands is one of the best ways to
stay healthy.

Use hand sanitizer
A little pocket bottle of sanitizer in your purse or
pocket can allow you to quickly sanitize your hands
before eating a meal, without the hassle of running
across the restaurant to the restroom.

Eat Right
Steer clear of sodas, sports drinks, fast food and
other junk. That stuff is okay once a week but not to
consume everyday. Eating stuff like that is what
causes obesity and diabetes.
Eat healthy, whole foods. Eggs, milk, veggies, fruit,
nuts, beans, and grains.
Keep your diet full of fruits and veggies. Limit the
meat intake as eating large amounts of meat or
eggs on a daily basis is bad for your health and
increases your cancer risk.

Brush your teeth
Dental hygiene saves you money by not having to
go to the dentist for rotten tooth extractions. You
also can contract gum disease by not caring for
your teeth properly.

Always disinfect minor cuts or wounds
No matter how small, there is a chance that a
wound can become infected and lead to much
worse problems down the line. Disinfect the wound
with alcohol or peroxide and bandage it properly.

Visit the doctor
You'll want to visit your doctor at least twice a year
anyway, for check-ups and routine exams. You'll
also want to go as soon as possible if any strange
symptoms appear.

Basic medicine cabinet necessities
- *Benadryl*
- *Ibuprofen*
- *Hydrogen Peroxide*
- *Bandaids*
- *Rubbing alcohol*
- *Diotame (nausea, heartburn, indigestion, upset stomach, anti-diarrheal)*
- *Cough drops*
- *Sinus pain & pressure*
- *Guaicon DMS (Cough suppressant)*

Income without a Job

Pallet business
If you're going to start any kind of business first and foremost, you're going to want a business license from big brother at your local courthouse or clerk. If you don't know where to get a license, call your local sheriff.

Pallets can be made by one person and you can sell them for $8-$12 a piece. Sell them to local factories and other places that use wood pallets. Some factories give away their broken ones for free, and all you have to do is repair them at that point. You'll need a trailer at that point to haul your load.
Most factories want at least 25-50 pallets a week, so if you can meet that quota weekly you'll be making a large amount of money at the end of each week. If you get behind on production, consider hiring help. You can run this business from the comfort of your own home or a small garden shed. Where you store your pallets safely are up to you.

Make things by hand and sell them
Sites like Etsy and Ebay are good places to make and sell handmade items for quick cash. This is a very common practice and people tend to buy a great deal of items. It's hard to get your product seen out there as it can get lost among the thousands of other people's products.

If yours are unique then you'll have less trouble appealing to the crowd looking for that type of necklace or jewelry. (Handmade jewelry sells the most it seems.)

Another idea is to make and sell candles by hand. Crisco and essential oils as well as mason jars work best for easy candle making profit.
Place ads in your local paper for a price, or start by taking samples of your candles to work and show to your coworkers. Strike a deal with them if they are interested in buying them, and they will likely buy some from you and spread the word of your business. You'll quickly make a profit if you sell it right.

Panhandlers (Don't trust em)
I never did this personally, I find it a very low-life way to make cash. It's dishonest in its nature and I've sat and watched panhandlers fool well over a hundred people in a few hours.

These con artists dress up as a homeless person (backpack, garbage strewn about, dirty appearance) and beg for money at the side of roadways and sidewalks. They often prey about supermarket parking lot exits/entrances, and they make damn good money doing it. Easily $500-$1000 dollars over a course of a week.
It's a shame to see people like that fooling good hearted people.

If by any means you find yourself in a legit and desperate need for money, this could work for you too. It is illegal however (probably mainly because it's nontaxable, but also dishonest) so take note of that. Also, next time you see a panhandler, don't fall for their pity trip signs and forlorn looks. They are trying to con you.

Actual homeless people don't usually beg from others as they know how to survive without money and don't need it. If you want to help the homeless, provide food and water as well as blankets and clothing. Those who want the cash are up to no good.

A license or nah?

You'll need a business license for any of these if they are your main source of income (minus panhandling) as they are considered no longer a hobby but a business.

If they are not your only source of income then it can be considered a hobby and does not require a license. (I'm not a lawyer, so check your laws)

You'll have to pay taxes if you make over a certain amount. (Check local laws)

Do an odd job

Often helping neighbors or mowing someone's lawn can result in cash. Strike up a deal, or do farm work as tobacco crop is another way to make money.

Save money on Losing Weight

No need for a gym membership
If you want to get out of the house and be around
other people in an air conditioned and motivating
environment, then the gym is right for you.
If you don't care about all that, can't afford it, or just
don't live near a gym, then you can learn to workout
at home or nearly anywhere you go.
You'll save money and get fit!
Plus, you could just make your own gym at home in
a room if you wanted to.

**ALWAYS STRETCH AND WARM UP BEFORE
ANY EXERCISE TO REDUCE THE RISK OF
TEARING OR PULLING MUSCLES.**

**DON'T EXERCISE IF YOU HAVE A HEART
CONDITION OR OTHER ILLNESS.**

Workout anywhere
- In your yard
- At home
- At parks
- Anywhere
- Jogging
- Calisthenics

How to gain muscle

- *Eat a lot of calories (2,500 - 3,000) a day*

Many guys out there these days are under the notion that if they only lift weights they'll get big and strong.

The reality is that if you only lift weights, the only thing you'll get is well-toned. If you want to gain mass and get stronger, you need to eat a lot of calories every day. The best way to do this is eat whatever you want to eat (whole foods like tuna and eggs are best alongside fruits and vegetables) and lift weights for several hours a day and then get adequate sleep. (8+ hours a night)

Skip the protein shakes and supplements. 3 square meals a day and consistency combined with adequate rest is the best way to get results.
Too much protein is hard on the kidneys and liver, don't consume large amounts of it in one sitting.
Be sure and drink plenty of water daily.

You then must let those muscles rest for a day or two until the soreness goes away before working out in the same fashion again.
Keeping track of your workouts on a notepad will help you stay consistent. Mix your routine up occasionally to stimulate your muscles.

Don't do the same old workout every single time.
Lift heavier weights (not too heavy, just by like 10 lbs more or so) and gradually add more weights as the weeks go by.

From my experience, I was adding 10 more pounds of weight every two weeks until I was benching 220 lbs. I started at 110 lbs.
Consistency therefore is key.

- *Get adequate rest*
After a long work out, you'll want to eat a decent meal and drink plenty of water. Now begins the fun process of resting and eating for the next two-three days. You'll want to get 8-10 hours of sleep at night and nap occasionally when you feel you need it. Try not to lift weights during this two-three day period if you are sore, as you could tear a muscle or worse.

If you're not sore, your muscles are likely not repairing themselves and so it's best to wait one day between workouts, and then hit the gym again. You have two options to get sore: work out longer or do different, more challenging workouts.
Eat. Sleep. Workout. Rest. Repeat.
That's the plan.

How to lose weight

- *Caloric intake needs to be lower than daily requirement:*

That is to say that according to the professionals, a woman needs at least 2,000 calories a day and a man needs 2,500.

If you eat less than your daily caloric requirements, your body pulls from its fat reserves to meet the lack of calories. Over time, this leads to weight loss. Exercising creates an even greater drain on your caloric reserves (fat), especially if you are not meeting your daily caloric requirement.

Please realize, that there are numerous factors to your calorie reserves that could raise or lower the caloric requirement.

If you have a slow metabolism, it will take even longer for you to see weight loss results, and you'll need even less daily calories.

-It takes at least two weeks of dieting to see results. There is no such thing as that "lose weight in 5 days" nonsense. That's not how the body works.

Stick to your diet for the rest of your life: people go about dieting and losing weight all wrong. You can't just up and eat produce and veggies for 6 months until you lose all the weight and then jump right back to your old ways, that's absurd! You'll just gain the weight right back.

Whenever you change your diet, your diet stays that way completely.

People get discouraged because they eat right for
two weeks and don't see any changes, but the
reality of it is that it takes two weeks of dieting **AND**
exercise to lose weight and see results.

If you simply diet, it will take a long time to get
results, and if you only exercise: you can't outrun
your fork. Too many calories over the daily calorie
requirement = weight gain. Plain and simple.

Keep track of your calories, try not to meet the daily
caloric requirement and keep up the cardio and you
will see the results. Even if it takes two months,
you'll see results*.
That's all up to you though.
Once you get down to the weight you are
comfortable with, you'll still have to watch calories if
you are to maintain your body weight.
Eat healthy and everything will fall into place.

Improvised weights

Guys in prison use improvised weights and so can you!

- Fill backpacks with books and do push ups or pull ups
- Fill garbage bags with water and lift them
- Place heavy objects in a bag and lift with them.
- Do curls with gallons of milk, bags of fruit, etc.
- Go out in the woods and move around heavy sticks.
- Move around heavy objects in your yard
- Carry heavy items

Nearly everything around you can be used to get bigger and stronger.

***Results depend on you!**

WHEN EXERCISING: STOP EXERCISING IF YOU FEEL FAINT OR DIZZY. GO SEE A DOCTOR ABOUT YOUR SYMPTOMS IMMEDIATELY.

Disclaimer: I am not a doctor or medical practitioner, therefore I cannot give sound advice on dieting and weight loss.
This advice is just from my own personal experience.

Passive Income

Make money online?
You sure can!
Tired of working that same old forty hour work week? Tired of trying to make ends meet, and only when you do, you realize that you'll have to start all over again next Monday?

What is passive income?
Passive income is money that you make by simply living your everyday life. You can be crossing the street and earning money. You could be eating breakfast and make a dollar. You could even be safely tucked away in your bed, all the while making cash.

What's the secret?
Why, passive income! If you want to make passive income, the best way to get started is to find a niche and go for it. Nothing is holding you back but yourself. You want to get rich, you want to live the dream; my friend, there is no dream working a dead end job and being away from your loved ones every single day for the next forty years.
If you want to see results, you've got to take action for one. Passive income is hard to get started, and it takes a while to get off the ground. Once it does though, you'll be bringing in thousands of dollars a month all while simply enjoying a cup of coffee with your spouse. All you have to do is find what you're good at, and go for it. There is money to be made,

that much is for certain.

So how do we quit our jobs?
By starting your passive income. You can't just up
and quit your job yet, you have to build your
empire. You have to have enough money coming in
that you can comfortably quit your job. It's a
gamble, in today's industry, as trends and other
markets are constantly changing. Demands rise
and fall, just like everything else. To generate
income, you likely have all you need right in your
very own home.
A computer with an internet connection.
It's true. It was always an option you had available.
It's the twenty first century though, and if you don't
want to work a forty hour week, you don't have to.
There are markets out there, opportunities for
endless cash flow. All you have to do these days is
reach for it and with a little hard work and diligence,
you'll get it!

What options are out there?
Ebooks, surveys, blogging, website building, ad
revenue, mobile app marketing, self-publishing,
there are so many!
Everyday, more and more people are tossing their
old 9 to 5 behind them and sleeping in an extra few
hours just by devoting a little hard work in front of a
computer screen. Sounds too good to be true?
It's not, if you're willing to dedicate the time and
effort to making money. You've likely done it all
these years with your current job, why not generate
a few more now while at home so that you can free
yourself of your chains?

Making money from home isn't easy; but like I said:
you'll have to make sure your passive income is off
the ground and generating money for you to be
able to say goodbye to the old grind.
Don't just up and drop your career and go buy a
computer: because getting rich overnight is not a
guarantee. (It has happened, though!)
You really wouldn't want to be in the unemployment
line struggling to eat.
Instead, you'll want to work a couple hours every
night after work on your chosen passive income
trade, and continue your daily life.
Eventually, you'll make money. It might be only a
little at first, but you'll make it.
Depending on your chosen area, your effort, and
your patience, you very well could become a
millionaire through passive income.

One more thing…
You should know that passive income does require occasional maintenance. If you get into one of the chosen trades I'll speak a little bit more about in a minute, you'll have to maintain it.
What that means is that if you start an entertainment channel on YouTube, people are going to expect you to upload videos once or twice a week. You can't just get rich overnight by putting in minimum effort and expect to not have to do anything else for the rest of your life.

That would be like an author publishing a best seller, and then for the rest of his life think that they don't have to write anymore because they published one book already. The cash flow will diminish for you, and you can't have that!
Especially not if you're relying on passive income. The best option is to get out there, decide what you want, and go for it.
Don't think that you can't do it, because you can. I am living proof of that. You can do anything you set your mind to; you just have to be willing to give it everything you've got to see it come true.

Work hard and success is inevitable!

1. **YouTube Channel**

This should be obvious by now. The fame of
YouTube and all it's glory can easily lead
you down the road of success.
YouTubers are known for their incredible
fortune accrued through online
entertainment.
Many more popular YouTube stars have
millions upon millions of dollars and the
cash just keeps pouring in.

What's the Secret?
Advertisements, self-promotion, sponsors,
Patreon and clever marketing. It's probably
one of the more "full time jobs" on this list,
as you still work from home but nonetheless
are still working.

To get people's attention you need to stand
out. These days it's getting harder and
harder to be original on YouTube as the
internet giant has grown significantly over
the past decade. It now is estimated that
there are more videos watched daily than
Google searches. Incredible, right?

YouTube has this thing called
advertisements, and what this means is that
you get paid for someone viewing an
advertisement on one of your videos. You

get paid on varying factors, usually advertisers don't pay though unless you watch their ads for at least thirty seconds or someone clicks on an ad.
YouTube changed their terms recently, and you can no longer instantly monetize your content. Rather you have to build up at least 1,000 subscribers or 10,000 views.

YouTube is a great way to start earning passive income. The downside is that it takes anywhere from 6 months to several years to make a large amount of money. You have to really love what you do, but if you work hard and develop a fan base, you can gain success.

Self-Promotion is getting your name out there. Interacting with your fans through social media such as Twitter, Facebook, and Twitch. Sharing your videos on social media sites is another way to generate money. More views equal more dollars.
Sponsors are companies that pay you to represent or review their product. They pay you depending on several factors, usually you have to contact them to see if they will allow you to sponsor them.
Patreon is a site which allows your followers to help support you monthly. It's like a donation site, except for everyday people. Your fans give you money to help

support you so you can keep making more content.

Marketing is done through sharing products that you've made with your fans. A major example of this is Teespring, which is a website that allows you to design and sell T-shirts; they do all the rest. They'll sell your shirts and you'll get a certain amount of profits. There are numerous other ways to market, ranging from selling your own designed products to art and much more.

2. Start your own Website

Through certain sites, you can set up a website and it allows you to use adsense to generate revenue.

Your own website is, next to YouTube, one of the best kept secrets of the passive income world.

You generate income by the people coming to your website and viewing your ads. There are other reasons for choosing to make your own website beyond just making money. It can be a blog about a particular hobby you like. It can be a website about your favorite recipes. Your imagination is the limiting factor here.

What's the secret?
To start your own website you'll need a

domain name for starters.

(Domain names are whatever you want to name your site)

Next is designing your website and content managing. That's where another outside source like Wordpress comes in handy.

From writing product reviews, affiliate marketing, sponsorships, Adsense, and selling your own products, the ways of making money are almost endless with a website.

Your website will be kind of bare at first, so your first step will be to decorate the site to be more inviting for people who view it but also convey the uniqueness about you.

Next, you'll need to promote your new website via social media.

I'll leave the rest for you to look into, should you decide to pursue making your own website.

Remember, the key to making good revenue off of a website is the traffic that the site gets. Invite people to your website after you've set up.

Then, consider researching how to affiliate market. It's the second best way to produce income for your site, and Amazon has their own site just for that.

3. Blogging

We're not talking blogging on Google blogger either. Just like starting a website, blogging is a great source of income. Tools like Adsense can be used here as well as other strategies used for website creation. Blogging takes a little bit of work to amass followers and get off of the ground, but it's not uncommon for people to replace their entire income with blogging.
You can get really creative with your blogs, and make them like miniature journals of things you love to do.
You really have to have a passion for blogging because it does take awhile to take off.
You have to get your name out there; let people see that you have a blog. You want to make your blog different and unique in order to gain people's interest in viewing it. They need to view your blog in order for you to profit from it.
Again, you can take to social media and post links to your blogs, amass followers and make some cash. You can create a lot of following for your blog from using social media alone.

4. Affiliate Marketing

Once you have a link to a product on Amazon that you like, you can post it somewhere on your blog, ebook, or website and recommend others to buy it.
Just like I've done up above with the YouTube equipment.

Whenever somebody clicks that link and actually purchases the product, you receive a share of the sale.
The percentage could be very low, but over time you can see what might happen if 300 or 1,000 people click the link and buy the product.
You guessed it, you'll get a percentage of each individual sale.
Quite a way to make money, wouldn't you agree?
In fact, it's one of the most recommended ways to make money. Just search "Affiliate marketing" on any search engine and review the results. There are countless websites out there willing to pay you cash just by placing links on your site.

5. Fiverr

If you don't mind writing, or being a "writer for hire", Fiverr is a freelance services market where authors can go and find work. Have you ever dreamed of becoming a writer? This is your chance.
You can literally pay the bills by doing odd freelance jobs. People will pay you to write for them.
There are numerous different jobs on Fiverr, not all related to writing. Some of them are for translating documents to other languages. You can do graphic design, animations, anything that you feel you're good at and can get paid to do.
Simply create an account on Fiverr, and advertise your expertise. Someone will likely hire your services and you can get paid.

6. Self-Publishing

Another great way to make a little income on the side is to publish Ebooks.
Ebooks are electronic books that are sold to be viewed on mobile devices (such as Kindles, phones, tablets and Nooks) and are often quite cheap compared to their physical paper counterparts.

So many people dream of writing books and becoming an author. Many try the traditional route to get published and never succeed. Luckily, we live in a time where childhood dreams can finally come true.
If you want to write, all you need is text editor like Google Docs or Microsoft Word, an account with Self Publishing KDP, and a little creativity.
With a little effort, you can produce as many books as you like and make some income on the side.
As a bonus, once the book is published, it will be on the Kindle store for years and years, allowing you to make money off of it for a long period of time.
The royalties for partnering with Amazon in KDP can be up to 70% of your asking price. That is quite a bit of money compared to most other self publishing places.
You should note, though, that despite it being easy to start your account and publish

books. Making money from Ebooks can sometimes seem really challenging as it's hard to get your name out there. People don't see your book as it gets lost among the millions of books on the internet.
Being an author is not an easy job, I can attest to that; but you should not give up.

There will be weeks that drag on and you don't make a single sale. You just have to hope somebody buys your work and pray for the best.
Many success stories can be found about e-book authors on Amazon. There's many books out there that made their authors chunks of money.

Then there's the reality of a starting author: You'll spend countless hours writing book after book, with not a single one of them ever being bought once.
You shouldn't be disheartened though, just write because you love to.
Do it because that's what the little kid you once were wanted to do when they grew up.
Do it because it was always your dream.
Do it, and forget about the money.
The money will come in it's own time.

7. Selling photos

Do you have a passion for photography?
You could potentially make a living by
selling photos on online sites.
There, you'll be able to make some extra
cash for simply taking pictures. It's not one
of the greatest options out there for passive
income, but if you have a passion for it, or a
ton of nice photos, there is someone out
there willing to buy them.

All you need is your cell phone camera, an
account, and a place to snap photos.

8. Making mobile apps

Remember 'Flappy Bird'? That game everybody was crazy about and made so many replicas of? Yeah, that one.
The bird and the pipes. Well, did you know it was estimated that the app alone brought in nearly _$50,000_ a day? Wow.
The Google Play Store is one of the largest app markets in the world, with thousands upon thousands of downloads daily.
With Google Admob, the potential to generate a lot of cash is right there in your hand.
"Well, I don't know how to code."
You don't have to know. There are apps out there like that allows you to make games without any coding knowledge whatsoever.

At that point you'll be a game dev. You can build a game, publish it to the Google Play store, and be making daily ad revenue. It's absolutely incredible. Honestly though, what's a few hours of your life getting used to using software that could potentially make you thousands of dollars a day?
Mobile gaming is a popular market, and you could be one of those developers out there dominating that market.

You will have to invest a little money, that is true, but think of the potential earnings you could make one day. The possibilities are out there. And, in the end, spending a little money would be worth earning more money.

9. Ebay

Ebay has been around for a very long time. It's still to this day a good way to make some cash off of something you own and no longer want. Simply log on, create an account, and list whatever it is you're wanting to sell.
You're your own business on Ebay. You post the item for sell, receive the order, and then send it out. There is no middle man; it's just the product, the customer, and you.

You could make it a job at home, where you'll buy items in bulk and on sale, and then sell them online for a profit.
While not necessarily passive income, if you were looking to make a full time job out of it, the potential is there.
It would require you to constantly be on the lookout for fresh deals and items that could potentially sell, but you could do it.

You'd basically become your own personal store, right from home.

10. Twitch Streaming

Do you like playing video games? Good news, there's potential to earn money there. You could stream yourself on Twitch and receive donations. You could be getting paid to do what you love, all from the comfort of your own home.

Twitch can be used alongside Google Adsense to generate ad revenue. Not only that, you can launch ads in your stream, whenever you need a restroom break/food break, further increasing your revenue.
You can make some serious cash through Twitch streaming if you have a large enough fanbase. I personally don't use Twitch, yet have heard alot of success stories about it. I knew I had to include it in this book

That's it.
As I said earlier, there are so many more ways to make income using nothing more than your computer. I've tried my best to limit it to the simplest and most profitable options to the best of my knowledge.
You can make money online, all you have to do is be able to work a computer and use a little old fashioned creativity, and you're on your way.

As a little disclaimer, I am not sponsored by any of these recommendations.

The Art of Free and Recycling

Where to find free stuff?
Free stuff is everywhere. I used to walk through restaurant drive-thrus after closing and pick up change for free money. Store parking lots and checkout areas were another area I scoured for free change. I made several dollars over the course of just one month by visiting several of my hotspots nightly.

I used to smoke when I was homeless to help with hunger pangs. I found that if you ask someone who is smoking for a cigarette, they'll give you one happily and for free.
Other free things, like napkins, condiments, and utensils can be obtained from restaurants by simply asking for them.
Save them, and they gradually add up.
Gas stations often provide free condiments or napkins (even coffee creamers and sugar). You can save those up as well.

Free grocery bags can often be found in garbage cans outside of stores. I often double bag my groceries not only for extra strength and so my groceries don't fall out, but that's extra bags for me at home.

Free water either hot or cold can be had at most restaurants, though these days many of them have started charging people for the container.
Once when I found out that I was being charged for water, I drove out of the drive-thru and to another restaurant where I new I could get it free.

Just don't get greedy. Take what you need and only a little of what you don't.

Dumpsters and free stuff
As mentioned previously, dumpsters are your #1 go to for free produce, food, clothing, electronics and all sorts of other goodies. Avoid restaurant dumpsters, as there is nothing to be found in there but rotten food and bacteria. Apartment or individual dumpsters may have needles or broken glass.
The best dumpsters I've found belonged to stores that did not serve any produce.

If you go dumpster diving, be sure and check your local laws, wear gloves, and bring a flashlight.
Also, dumpster diving is dangerous and therefore proceed at your own risk.

Strolling through the park
I recently found a sleeping bag that someone had abandoned in a local park. Its original price was well over $100+ to my surprise. I took it home, washed it and now keep it for my own usage.
Avoid strange bags and tennis balls though.

Garbage night

People throw out all kinds of good and still salvageable items. Drive through your local area on garbage night and look for furniture or other goodies on the stoop.

Free Internet

Several locations offer free internet, so if you're out and about with your laptop or phone and don't have any service, locate a place with free Wifi and connect.
Good places to look for free internet are local libraries, gyms, restaurants and coffee shops.

Recycling

Reuse items like butter containers, whipped cream bowls, pickle jars, coffee cans and other such items for both free storage bowls and dishware.
Plastic forks and other utensils can be washed and reused over and over again. Even if they break, you can pick one up from somewhere free.

Plastic grocery bags can be used for all sorts of tasks, from garbage bags, to improvised waterproof socks, disposable gloves, and can be ripped in strips to make cordage. When I was hitchhiking I had tied a cardboard sign to my backpack that said "God Bless" using nothing more than handmade cord made from a grocery bag.

Improvising a cutting tool

Often times you'll find yourself needing a cutting tool but not having one. It can be a troublesome experience if you don't carry an actual knife. These situations tend to occur when you've just arrived at a hotel and you're too tired to deal with shopping. Instead of buying one, why not make one? Chances are, if you don't have a knife or scissors, you might have a disposable razor. I learned this trick when I was homeless, and often I didn't have a knife on hand as I didn't want to waste money on one.

All you have to do is "pop a razor" by pushing the corner of it's head against a table or hard surface. The result will be that usually if you do it right, the head will pop and the paper thin little blades will come out. Then I would take a lighter (do this in a well ventilated area) and light the head of the razor on fire while holding the razor blade against the handle. I would expose just the edge of the razor a little past the edge of the handle and then touch where the blade and handle meet with the melting plastic. The result is like hot gluing the blade to the razor handle. You have to be very careful doing this, as it's easy to get cut, burnt by melting plastic, or inhaling the toxic fumes from the melting plastic. Whatever you do, don't do this indoors, and don't breathe the fumes. They're toxic and carcinogenic. Other alternatives are that you can superglue the blade to a pencil, a stick, a pen, or the razor handle itself. Either way, be extremely cautious not to cut yourself. Those razors are incredibly sharp, and one wrong move could fillet a finger.

I would use my razor knife on the road for a wide variety of tasks. I would cut open packages, cut string, cut cardboard and basically everything you can do with a standard knife. To re sharpen it I would use the same sharpening method you would use on a knife, but I would use my leather belt or if I was wearing denim I would use it to sharpen my razor. The beauty of these razors is that you get a great deal of homemade knives and can shave your face for only a couple dollars. Out there, the improvised razor knife saved my life and made life on the street a little bit easier. I still remember using it to cut open

garbage bags in the middle of a cold winter night trying to find something to eat.
I initially didn't want to include this in this book in fear some naive kids might try it, but I realize that if someone was to become homeless, that this improvised knife could save their life.
Therefore I decided it best to include it.

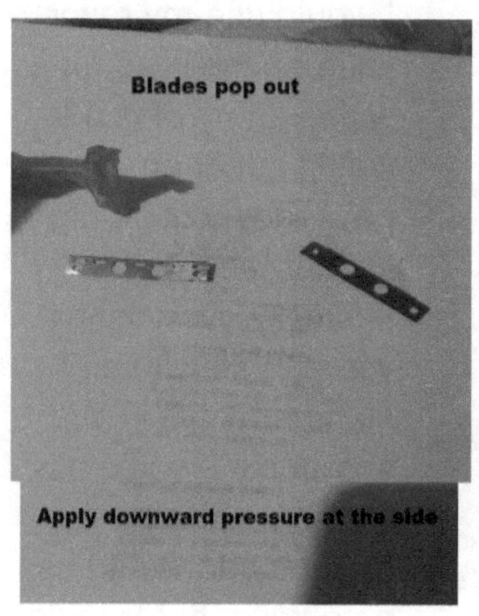

Cordage

is a necessity when you're homeless. What was once a common and everyday item is a luxury when homeless. Cordage can be used to make everything from large rope, to securing your shoes, to lashing two sticks together. Cordage is the glue holding your life together out in the streets.
From simply using strong roots or plastic bag strips, to handmade cordage from grass and bark, cordage is a skill that is easy to learn and would be able to help you to survive.

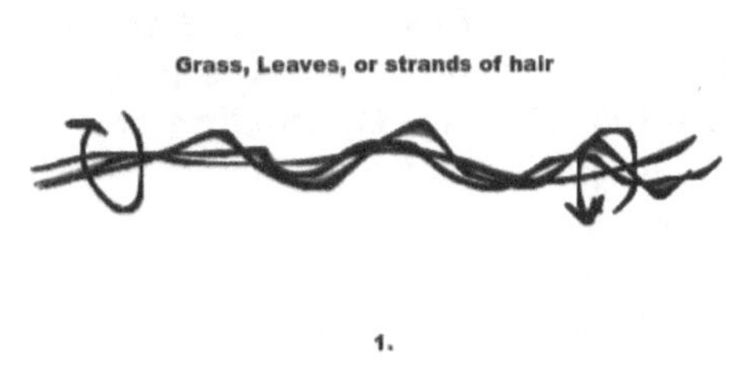

Roll each end extremely tight by rotating either end opposite directions. This method is called reverse-wrap cordage.

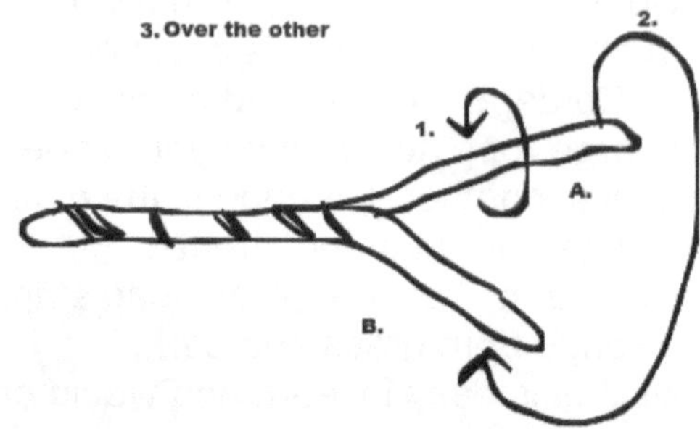

Rotate (A) away from you tightly (Step 1.), Then pull (A) over (B) in (Step 2.). When properly done, (A) piece will take the position of (B) piece in diagram, and vice versa. Maintain pressure on (A) after rolling, and the rotating (A) into (B) position and then pulling (B) up into (A) position.

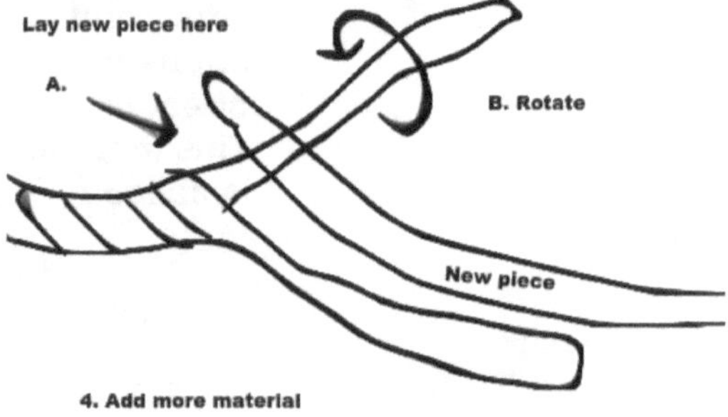

When adding new material, pinch the new piece at the crotch of the split firmly, the rotate (B) and twist downwards. Essentially working the new piece into the cordage. Repeat this method every time you run out of material to twist, until you have desired length of cordage necessary.

2 ply

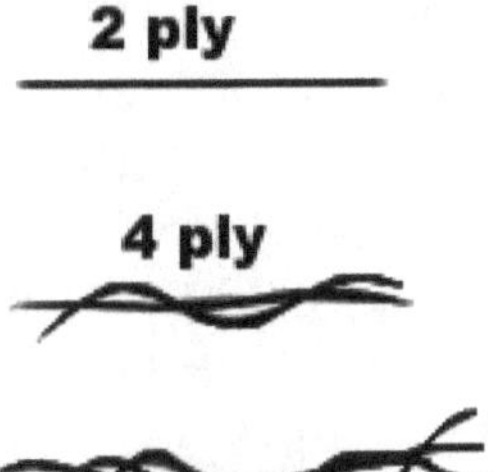

4 ply

6 ply

2 ply is made by reverse wrapping cordage with one strand. 4 ply is made with two strands at a time, 6 with 3, etc. You can make as much as 12 ply if you have the resources.

Fire from AA batteries/Cell phone

That's right. Even without a lighter or any other gear, you've likely got your cell phone on you. While it's not recommended to tear your phone apart straight away just for a fire. If you've no service and the battery dies, it still might have enough juice to ignite some tinder. If failure to ignite, battery can be punctured to cause fire. Be sure and keep hands free of battery when doing this as injury can occur. **Caution: Smoke will be Toxic. Do not breathe it.**

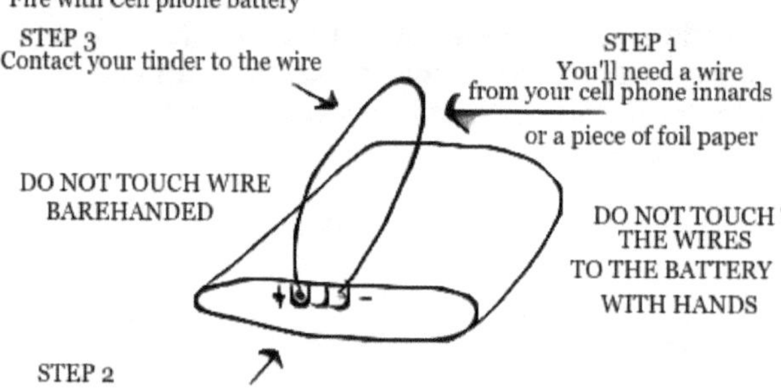

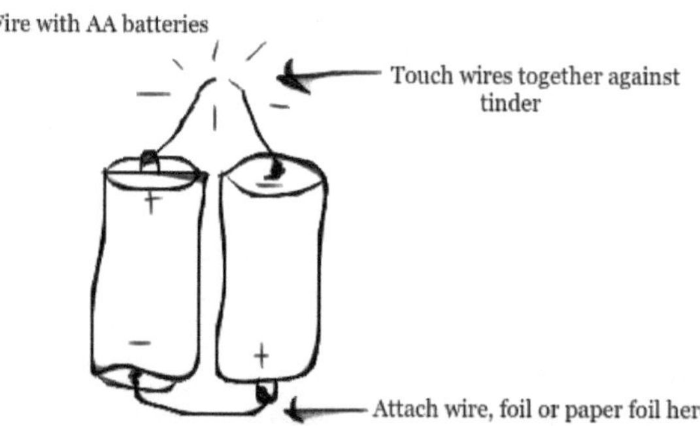

Fire with AA batteries or cell phone batteries SHOULD NOT be attempted indoors.
WARNING: DO NOT TOUCH CONTACT WIRES ON

EITHER BATTERY BAREHANDED. BURN HAZARD. SECURE THE WIRE BATTERIES WITH PINE RESIN, OR TAPE IF YOU HAVE IT.

AA Battery Lighter

Another one of those items that I didn't want kids to know about or include in this book. Out there on the street, you often can't afford to spend money on a lighter or some other item you can't afford. I used this method by using the blades from a razor secured by melting the handle and using the melted plastic to dab the blades and hold them to the batteries. You then break the second razor in half and glue each piece on the opposite end of each battery. You then touch the broken blades together and where they make contact will get incredibly hot, allowing you to touch it to dry grass or a cigarette to light it.

You will get burnt if you are not careful.

Be sure not to touch the blades when you do this.

Fire can save your life on a cold winter night, and especially if you're homeless. Therefore I thought it best to include this method.

Homesteading On Breadcrumbs

What is homesteading?
If you ever find yourself wanting to live a simpler life and tired of the humdrum 9 to 5 and the mind numbing advertisements from constant consumerism based capitalism, then homesteading is for you.
So what is it? Basically your home becomes your livelihood. Your home provides all of your necessities; you don't rely on the utility companies in any form, and your life is much like that of the amish. You'll provide your own water, grow your own food and probably use an outhouse.
Now, there are two ways to go about homesteading. You either start out with a lot of money and you want to go fancy with solar power and pre drilled wells, or you start out with nothing but a small half-acre of land passed down to you from a family member.
Either way, you're going to need some land.

Homesteading can be incredibly cheap. I've heard of people living on less than $1,000 a year just from it. It's the next best option to squatting or living in a car. The problem usually lies in finding a rural plot of land which allows you to live in solitude and away from the busy highway with it's booming bass vehicles and barking dogs.
You need land

Less than an acre these days costs somewhere
from $250-$1000 depending on the state and
location in which the land is. Obviously the desert is
going to have the cheapest land.
You'll want your own land because that way,
nobody can tell you what you can and cannot do on
your own property. I highly doubt someone you're
renting from is going to allow you to dig a well and
outhouse hole on their property.
You don't need a ranch and you don't need 2000
sq acres of property.
To support a small family, all you need is an acre or
less. There are websites out there that sell cheap
property in America that you can purchase without
even seeing it physically. You can move your family
literally overnight to the site.
You can do all this without even seeing the land,
but I would advise against it because in all honesty
you don't know what you're buying. I personally
wouldn't want to own land in Arizona if I didn't want
to live in the scorching heat of the arid desert.

You need a shelter
You could build it yourself, or it could be just a
small RV, Mini-camper, or a fixed up and insulated
shed (what they call tiny houses). Regardless of
what you call home, you could even build a small
A-Frame house which is rather cheap to build and
insulate. Even if you had nothing else, you could
live in your vehicle on the property. Nobody can tell
you that you cannot, it's your land. If you have
children, then the government might be able to say

something about your livelihood if you are living out of a vehicle.

If you have a home, then they will likely not bother you about your way of life. At any rate, don't go bragging or telling people you know about your life. Some states make it illegal to live in such a manner without utilities (big brother will pass any law if given enough money by corporations it seems) and you don't want to be forced back onto the grid if homesteading is your way of life.

You'll only have to pay annual taxes on your property if you play all of your cards right.

Water for free

For those on a budget, or who started homesteads without hardly any money, didn't have the luxury of solar water stills and solar power. Likely, they lived by candlelight/oil light and hand-dug wells.

For digging a well, you simply dig a hole in the ground down to underground water. There are tons of methods out there for finding the water, from "dowsing" to using electronic equipment. Some people make rain catchers, although big brother has outlawed this method.

Lighting

Oil lamps and candles provide most lighting needs, and are relatively cheap but also dangerous for those with butter fingers and rather clumsy. You can improvise both or make your own at home. DIY oil candles can be as simple as a piece of string sticking out of a small can with ¼ of cooking oil in the bottom of it. The string soaks up the oil and burns like a candle.

People have made giant candles with tubs of crisco. People have made their own cheap candles with mason jars and melted crisco and cotton strings.

Whatever route you take, you're saving much more money making your own than buying for the year.

Heating and Cooling

The luxury of air conditioning and electric furnaces are long gone when homesteading. Your main defense in both freezing and overheating situations is to rely on the insulation of your shelter. You can make cheap insulation by using shredded newspaper, but you'll need nearly 50 lbs or more depending on the size of your house.

During the **summer**, the best you can do for keeping cool is opening your windows and sitting outside in the shade. Fan yourself with a fan, use cool wet rags, dress lightly etc.

During **winter**, you'll likely use a wood stove for heating. Buying one is by far the more expensive option as a wood stove can range anywhere from $100-$1000 and weigh far beyond what one man can carry.

DIY Woodstove (Rocket Stove)

The second best option is to make your own wood stove using an 50 Gal oil drum. These are pretty common in rural and impoverished areas, as well as isolated areas where ingenuity and cold weather compete for survival, like rural Canada or Alaska.

Often, the people who live in those areas make due with what they have to survive, leading to ingenious ways of getting by and reaching their goals at obtaining their necessities.

The Oil drum wood stove is essentially just an oil drum that has been modified with a door and and a pipe to allow you to burn wood inside of it. If placed vertically they can also be cooked atop of. They have to be sat atop cinder blocks or a bed of gravel as they cannot rest directly on the floor of your abode lest they start a fire.

Under no circumstances should you rest the woodstove atop your floor. Buy cinder blocks if you have no other option. The exhaust pipe can be directed out of a window or through your roof.

Cooking

In the summer you'll be cooking outdoors more often than cooking indoors. It's best to do this on a grill or a fireplace somewhere outside that you have designated.

In the winter and cool months, you'll likely be cooking indoors on your woodstove. To bake things, you'll use a cover in conjunction with a trivet. Set the pan of food you wish to bake upon an iron trivet and cover with a large pot.

Bathing

As in the olden days, most of your baths will likely be indoors in a large metal tub. In the summer or warm climates year round, there are inexpensive camping showers that are basically black bags that you hang up and stand beneath.

In order to have hot water, you'll fill the tub with half cold water, and then after boiling water in a pot on the stove, add the boiling water slowly and gradually to the tub until the water is tolerable.

This is best done outdoors so that your bathwater can be dumped out afterwards.

Some people bathe with just a wash cloth and warm water. Whatever gets you clean is all that matters.

Washing Dishes
In the same way you make bathwater, you'll make dishwater in a small pot. In another pot or tub, you'll add cool water without anything in it (rinse water) and this is where you'll dip your dishes to rinse them.

For dish soap, you'll add 1 part vinegar to 3 parts of your dishwater. White distilled vinegar cuts grease and disinfects your dishes. It will be your dish soap. Once you've washed your dish, dip it in the rinse water and then set to dry.

Using the Restroom
Many homesteaders used to use the old outhouse, and while that's a good idea, rushing from the house to the outhouse is a constant pain in the side, plus wasp nests and spiders inside the outhouse.

You could go the "only have a water utility" route and have plumbing hooked up on your property. You can choose to use an outhouse, or a five gallon bucket. Whatever you decide is your choice.

Livestock
Most folks go out and buy a male cock and two or three hens to get started. The chickens will mate and rear up eggs that you can use for food. If you allow the eggs to hatch, you'll further increase your supply of chickens over the years. You can eat the chickens too (personally I'll just use the eggs). You can also raise rabbits and use them for meat. You

can feed the rabbits grass and clovers from your yard, or veggies from your garden. Chickens like seeds and grains, but will likely feed themselves if you turn them loose to graze.

Everything else seems to be too much cost to deal with (cows, pigs, goats, etc.) as they require more land and money to care for and purchase.

Gardening

You can raise a garden up depending on your location, and can the produce your rear from it. A large majority of your produce will come from your garden, you will not be buying it.

Tomatoes, corn, and green beans are great plants to start with. You can order any type of seeds you need through the internet (how to do that without electricity? I'll explain in a minute.)

What about a cellphone?

What about them? If you must have one, then you can still pay for your monthly plan. All you have to do for charging them is either while your car is running through a car charger, or a solar powered charger which is the best option.

Having internet access via cell phone allows you to order whatever you may need for your homestead.

The Slingshot for Survival and Sport

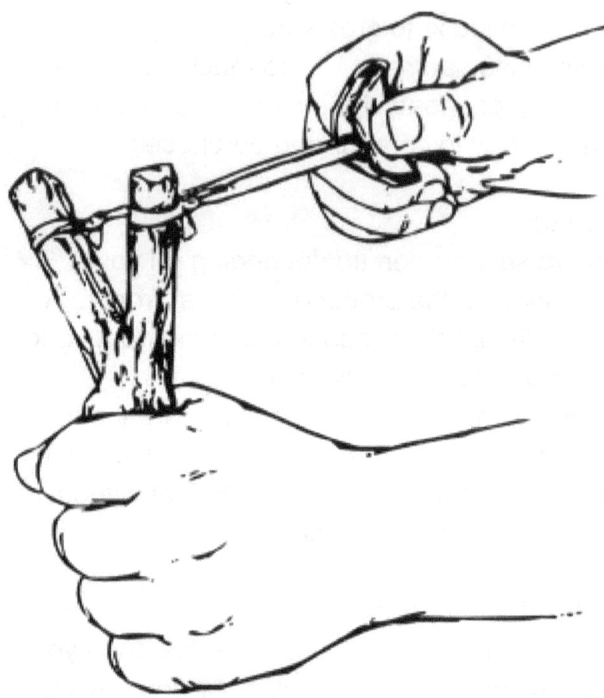

Slingshot History

Slingshots never existed prior to the economic collapse of the 1930's that left millions starving and without any money. Folks relied on the old ways to survive and the every crafty human ingenuity (that aided us to survive thousands of years) shone through to produce one of man's easiest to craft weapons in modern history.

Farmers and country boys alike set out without any ammo for their guns (or conserved it for home defense purposes) set out to take small game using nothing more than strips of inner tube, a piece of boot leather and a forked stick. All they had in their pockets for ammo was gravel rocks, or ball bearings for the more fortunate. Some melted down lead to mold spherical shot out of it, but a majority of people just hunted with gravel.

For nearly a decade, the slingshot harvested everything from small birds to rabbits and possums. Men fed their families and avoided starvation using this humble tool.

Nowadays, people regard the slingshot as some 1950's toy, but the reality of it is that it was never made for children but out of necessity to feed starving families. It was literally the alternative to the gun during it's time. Without the slingshot, thousands if not millions of families would have perished.

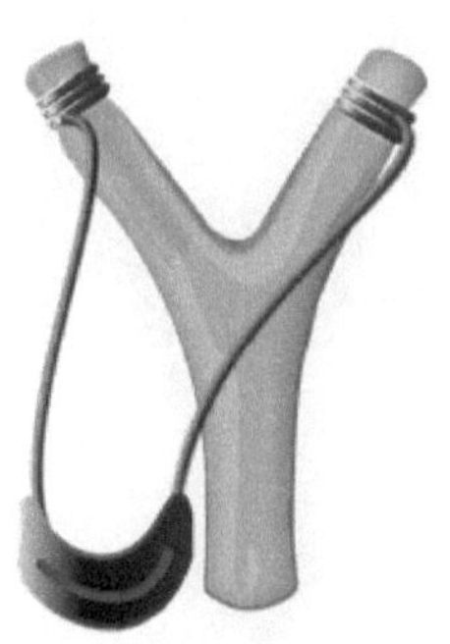

Remember that next time you see a slingshot. It's fully capable of killing.

Make your own
These days, you could fashion a slingshot out of any elastic material, a piece of leather, and a forked stick.
Fork: can be made out of bent metal, carabiners, or anything else. Mainly and traditionally what is most common is the fork of a tree.

Elastic: Office rubber bands, Chained rubber bands, Exercise bands, or motorcycle inner tubes can be used to make a slingshot band. (this is the part of the slingshot you'll likely pay money to obtain)

Pouch: Leather works best. You can find leather from old furniture, purses, old clothing, dress shoes etc. Check thrift stores for sources of leather clothing. Never pay for the high dollar stuff.

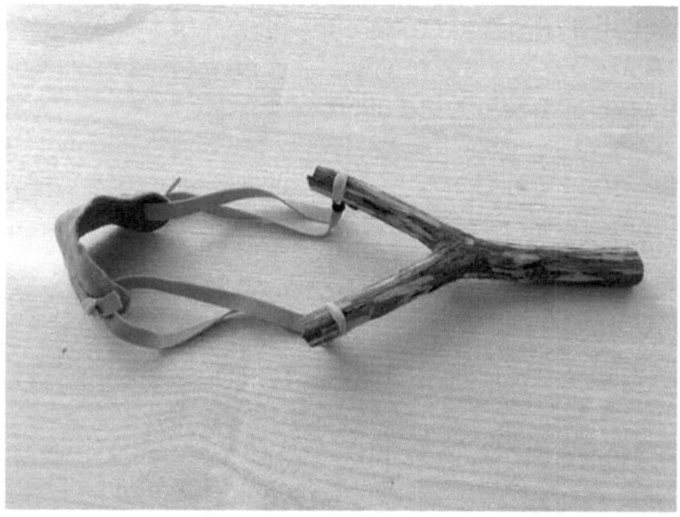

Frugal Troubleshooting

Is it dark in your house but daylight outside?
Open the blinds and save money on electricity.

Is it plugged in but not in use?
Unplug it. Phone chargers included.
(Unless it's a refrigerator or breathing machine of course.)

Is it cold in your house, but not freezing?
Wear more layers. Cover up with a blanket. Don't touch that thermostat, leave it at 68 -70 degrees F.

Did you do laundry on a sunny day?
Hang the clothes up outside. Save money on electricity by not using the dryer.

Did you do laundry on a rainy day?
Hang the clothes up inside. All you need is some type of rope/extension cord and some clothespins/hangers.

Don't have a dryer?
Hang the clothing up indoors/outdoors.

Don't have a washer?
Wash your clothes in the bathtub by hand. Do note that clothes washed by hand occasionally leak water, so you'll want to cover the floor below them with waterproof material; or just hang them over the bathtub.

Don't have dryer sheets?
Rolled up balls of aluminum work as a static
remover. Might scratch your dryer a little. You want
at least two. Vinegar on a rag works best.

Phone bill too high?
Try looking at other plans near you. Some cell
phone companies will actually reduce your plan if
you try to leave because you found a cheaper
option.

**Can't afford to pay rent on a vehicle, furniture,
or some other luxury?**
Return it to the dealer. If it's a vehicle, first replace
it with one that has been used. Always buy your
vehicles, *never* rent. Annual taxes are bad enough,
forget renting a vehicle, that's for people with
disposable income.
You will incur negative credit for returning a vehicle,
though.

Need to save money on heating/cooling?
Turn your thermostat to 68 F all year long. If it's
summer though, just open up the windows and put
a box fan facing inward to help cool things off and
give your thermostat a rest.

Want to get in shape but don't have a gym?
Workout at home; It's completely free. If you can't
rigorously exercise, then get up and clean your
house or do chores. That counts as exercise too.

Bored?
Go to the library. Read books. Play a board game.
Play cards. Do chores. Exercise. Take a nap. Visit
friends. Take a walk through the park. Listen to the
radio. Go fishing/hunting/hiking. Play with your
pet(s). Work in your garden. Clean up the yard. Go
sit on the stoop and people watch. Practice your
hobby.
DO NOT shop when bored.

Don't know how to repair something?
A lot of things can be repaired these days by
people who have never done it before all by doing
research. You should avoid fixing anything that is
electrical or dangerous to repair if you don't know
what you're doing. Ask around for cheap repairmen
in your area, either via neighbors or family. Cheap
appliances can be replaced without hassle.

**Can't see to write something down even with
the blinds open?**
Go closer to the window.

Someone's trying to talk to you while you're on your cell phone in public?
You should pay attention to your surroundings and put that phone down. That's dangerous, y'know.

Public Transportation too expensive?
Ride a bike or walk to get around. Doubles as free exercise. (I know that sometimes you have no choice but to use public transport.)

When considering groceries, are you out of something?
If the answer is yes or almost, put it on the list. If the answer is no, do not put it on the list.
This can save you hundreds in the long run.

Do you need new clothes?
Go to a Goodwill/Discount store/Thrift shop/Salvation Army. Never buy new clothing. New clothing and name brands are a waste of money.

Too ashamed to buy/wear used clothing?
Guess you bought the wrong book, huh?

Need new shoes, socks, or underwear?
These things you should never buy used, for sanitary purposes. Buy the least expensive shoes you can find, but also the most durable and comfortable. Sometimes paying high dollar for one pair of shoes that last several years is better than a cheap pair that last 3 months, but only if you can afford it.

Socks and underwear should *always* be generic.

See something you really *want* but don't *need*?
Don't buy it. Put it down and walk away. The next time you return to that store immediately put it in the cart before doing anything else.
You'll likely not want it by then. The logic here is that you might still want it, but you'll think long and hard while you're grocery shopping. Do you really *need* it, or just *want* it?

Prefer name brand over generic?
If you haven't realized by now that generic is the same product but a different label, I don't know what else to tell you.
When you buy name brand, you pay for the name and the advertisements; yet still get the same product for nearly double the money.
Buy generic, always.

Have too much stuff?
Sell it. Make a profit off of it, or at least recover a little money. If you don't use it, haven't used it in over a year, and it's not a tool of some kind, sell it.

Don't have the right tool for the job?
Improvise. Even large rocks can drive nails like a hammer. Scissors work as letter/package openers. Butter knives can be used as flathead screwdrivers. Take an object, and see how many uses you can get out of it.

Don't use an app but still pay for the subscription?
Cancel your subscription.

Problem not listed?
Read the book again. If that fails, consider using the internet to search for your answer.

The Frugal Shopping List

Groceries

- Dry powdered milk
-All purpose flour
-Old fashioned oats
-Black tea bags
-Bananas
-Russet potatoes
-Olive oil
-Salt
-Peanut butter
-Rice
-Dried or Canned beans
-Canned Fruit
-Apples
-Dried Peas
-Yellow onions

Cleaning supplies

- White distilled vinegar
- Hydrogen peroxide
- Baking Soda
- Lemon Juice
- Rubbing Alcohol
- Borax
- Dish soap (your choice)
- Washing Soda
- Salt
- Spray Bottles (1 for each cleaner)
- Permanent Marker (for labeling)
- A broom and dustpan

- *A mop*
- *Vacuum cleaner*
- *Microfiber cloth*
- *Garbage bags*

Hygiene

- *Toothbrush*
- *Bar soap (your choice)*
- *Baking Soda (For brushing your teeth)*
- *Disposable Razors*
- *Unscented Deodorant (Or your choice)*
- *Cotton swabs (for your ears)*
- *Feminine products (if applicable)*
- *Shampoo and Conditioner (if long hair applies)*
- *Emery Board*
- *Comb or brush (if applicable)*
- *Hair clipper set*

Healthcare
- *Diotame*
- *Guaicon DMS (cough suppressant)*
- *Ibuprofen*
- *Benadryl*
- *Cough drops*
- *Sinus pain pressure*
- *Bandaids*
- *(Whatever specific medicines you need)*

Office Supplies
- *Envelopes*
- *Stamps*
- *Pens and pencils*
- *Yellow legal pads*
- *Paper clips*
- *Scissors*
- *Thumb tacks*

House Items
- *Flashlight*
- *AA/AAA Batteries*
- *Matches*
- *Duct tape*
- *Hot glue sticks*
- *Simple hand tools*
- *Corded drill with a drill bit set*

Conclusion

That just about does it. I hope that you've learned how to live below your means. I'm grateful for you dear reader.

I wrote this guide in hopes that it would teach you how to provide for yourself and your family using very little money. I hope some people hear my story of homelessness and feel like they are capable of overcoming anything. I want to thank my grandparents for showing me how to survive in the world.

I've survived several years of both homelessness and living in my car. Through it I obtained my education, and worked my dream job.

I especially want to thank those that gave me a chance, but most importantly I want to thank my mother for showing me how to get by the best she knew how.

And thank you, grandfather in Illinois. Your words inspired this book.

May this book be a tribute to all of you through the years to come.